Ecce Romani
Language Activity
Book I

Fourth Edition

SAVVAS
LEARNING COMPANY

ISBN-13: 978-0-13-361119-9
ISBN-10:   0-13-361119-1

26 20

Two Roman Girls

In addition to vocabulary, the activities in this chapter focus on:
1. use of articles (*a, an, the*) when translating Latin.
2. translating Latin verbs in three different ways as in the vocabulary lists.
3. differences in word order between Latin and English.
4. identifying nouns, adjectives, and verbs.

Vocabulary

Activity 1a Vocabulary

*Study the vocabulary list on page 204 alone or with a partner. Note the arrangement of words
by part of speech: nouns, adjectives, and verbs.*

The Story

Activity 1b Articles in English Translations

Translate the following sentences into English:

1. Flāvia est puella Rōmāna.

_____

2. Flāvia est in pictūrā.

_____

3. Flāvia in vīllā habitat.

_____

What words have you included in your English translations that are not in the Latin?

_____ and _____

What are these words called?

_____

Activity 1c Translating Latin Verbs into English

Translate the following sentence three ways, using the different translations for verbs found in the vocabulary list in your textbook:

Puella Rōmāna sub arbore sedet.

1. _____

2. _____

3. _____

The words *is* and *does* in the phrases *is sitting* and *does sit* are called *helping verbs.*

Do the Latin sentences in the story in Chapter 1 of your textbook use this kind of verb? _____

How many times is the Latin verb **est** used in the story? _____

Is it a helping verb? _____

Translate the following into Latin:

1. The girl is reading. _____

2. The girl is sitting. _____

Activity 1d Word Order

Describe two ways in which the order of the words in the Latin sentence in Activity 1c differs from the order of the words in your three English translations of it:

1. _____

2. _____

Building the Meaning

Parts of Speech: Nouns, Adjectives, and Verbs

Activity 1e Parts of Speech: Nouns, Adjectives, and Verbs

Read the following story and identify the part of speech of the words in bold type. Put an N over the nouns, the letters ADJ over the adjectives, and a V over the verbs:

Flāvia in Italiā **habitat.** Etiam Cornēlia in Italiā habitat. Cornēlia iam in vīllā

rūsticā habitat. In **vīllā vīcīnā** habitat Flāvia. Cornēlia **legit** dum Flāvia **scrībit.**

Flāvia **est laeta** quod Cornēlia iam in **vīllā** habitat.

Applying What You Have Learned

Activity 1f Writing the Language

Translate the following English sentences into Latin. Include all long marks. Use the stories and vocabulary lists in your textbook, as well as the vocabulary lists in this book, to help you:

1. Who is sitting under the tree?

_____

2. A girl, named Cornelia, is now sitting under the tree and reading.

_____

3. Another girl, named Flavia, is writing.

_____

4. Why is Flavia writing?

_____

5. Flavia is writing because Cornelia is reading.

_____

Activity 1g Expanding Your English Vocabulary

Using the word bank on page 4, write the word that could replace the italicized word or words in each sentence or could complete a sentence. Use the Latin words in parentheses to help determine the meaning of the English words. Then write the English translation of each Latin word in the word bank:

1. Cornelia enjoys the *country* life of Baiae. _____

2. Flavia lives in the area surrounding Baiae.

    She lives in the _____ of Baiae. _____

3. The island was all rock; it was unfit for human *living*. _____

4. The old Roman senator dictates all his letters to a *person who writes them down*. _____

5. Writing letters is a job usually done when sitting.

    It is a _____ job. _____

6. Several candidates will be *named* to run in the next election. _____

7. The koala is a *tree-dwelling* animal. _____

8. Make sure your writing is clear and *readable*. _____

9. Camels often *live in* the desert. _____

10. Wine often leaves a *deposit that settles on the bottom of the glass.* _____

sediment (**sedet**) _____	legible (**legit**) _____
habitation (**habitat**) _____	vicinity (**vīcīna**) _____
nominated (**nōmine**) _____	arboreal (**arbore**) _____
rustic (**rūstica**)* _____	sedentary (**sedet**) _____
inhabit (**habitat**) _____	scribe (**scrībit**) _____

*This word is not given by itself in the vocabulary list for Chapter 1 in your textbook, but you should be able to provide a meaning for it.

When you are reading an English text and you see a word you do not know, look carefully to determine if it might be related to a Latin word you do know.

Activity 1h Reading Latin

Read the story, noting nouns, adjectives, and verbs and how the word order is different from English. Reread the story for comprehension. Then answer the questions that follow with complete Latin sentences:

At the Country House and Farm

Quis est puella Rōmāna? Puella Rōmāna est Cornēlia quae aestāte in vīllā rūsticā habitat. Cornēlia est laeta quod sub arbore legit. In vīllā vīcīnā habitat altera puella Rōmāna, nōmine Flāvia.

Later:

Cornēlia in vīllā sedet et legit. Ubi est Flāvia? Etiam Flāvia in vīllā sedet. Quid facit puella? Flāvia scrībit dum Cornēlia legit. Flāvia est laeta quod in vīllā sedet et scrībit.

1. Cūr est Cornēlia laeta?

_____

2. Quis in vīllā vīcīnā habitat?

_____

3. Quid facit Cornēlia in vīllā?

_____

4. Quid facit Flāvia in vīllā?

_____

A Summer Afternoon

In addition to vocabulary and the story, the activities in this chapter focus on:
1. adverbs, conjunctions, and interjections.
2. subjects, linking verbs, and complements.
3. **est** and **sunt** when used as linking verbs and when used without a complement.
4. singular and plural subjects and verbs.

Vocabulary

Activity 2a Parts of Speech

In Chapter 1, you were given definitions of nouns, adjectives, and verbs. Here are definitions of three more parts of speech with examples from the Latin words in Chapter 1. Give English meanings for the Latin words:

ADVERBS (ADV): words that modify verbs, adjectives, or other adverbs:

etiam _____

iam _____

CONJUNCTIONS (CONJ): words that link words, phrases, or clauses:

dum _____

et _____

quod _____

ubi _____

INTERJECTIONS (INTERJ): words that can stand alone and that call attention to a statement or express an emotion:

Ecce! _____

Activity 2b Vocabulary

Study the vocabulary list on page 205 alone or with a partner. Note that adverbs and conjunctions are grouped under their respective headings. Go to the corresponding list on the Companion website where you will find an additional list of adverbs and conjunctions you have met so far.

The Story

Activity 2c Comprehension

Using your understanding of the story in your textbook, complete the sentences below with the appropriate Latin phrases from the word bank. There are more phrases than you will need:

1. Cornelia and Flavia spend a lot of time together because _____.

2. They are tired of sitting under the tree so they _____.

3. Flavia keeps running because _____.

4. Cornelia and Flavia read and write _____.

5. Finally the girls _____.

in agrīs ambulant	ad vīllam rūsticam ambulant
in arbore sedet	sunt laetae
sunt amīcae	est puella strēnua
dum sub arbore sedent	est dēfessa

Building the Meaning

Subjects, Verbs, Linking Verbs, and Complements

Activity 2d Subjects, Linking Verbs, and Complements

Fill in the blanks in this story, following the English cues. Use each word or phrase in the word bank only once:

Puellae sunt (energetic) _____. (Today) _____

Flāvia et Cornēlia (in the fields) _____ **currunt.** (In a short time)

_____ _____ **puellae sunt dēfessae. Puellae nōn iam** (run)

_____. **Cornēlia est** (tired) _____. **Flāvia** (also)

_____ **est dēfessa.** (At last) _____ **Flāvia** sub

arbore sedet (but) _____ **Cornēlia** (to the country house)

_____ _____ ambulat.

sed	tandem
hodiē	currunt
strēnuae	brevī tempore
dēfessa	in agrīs
quoque	ad vīllam

Now, look at the story on page 7 and study the words in bold type. Put an S over each subject, an LV over each linking verb, and a C over each complement. Then put the letters ADV over each adverb and CONJ over each conjunction.

Activity 2e *Est* and *Sunt* as Linking Verbs and When Used without a Complement

Translate each sentence below and circle Linking Verb or No Complement as appropriate:

1. In agrīs est vīlla.   Linking Verb   No Complement

_____

2. Vīlla est Rōmāna.   Linking Verb   No Complement

_____

3. Est altera puella in pictūrā.   Linking Verb   No Complement

_____

4. Altera puella est Flāvia.   Linking Verb   No Complement

_____

5. Flāvia et Cornēlia sunt amīcae.   Linking Verb   No Complement

_____

Forms

Verbs: The Endings -*t* and -*nt*

Activity 2f Singular and Plural Subjects

The following words could be used in sentences as subjects. Write Sing. in the blank if a singular verb would be expected and Pl. if a plural verb:

1. amīca _____   **4.** vīlla _____   **7.** puella _____

2. puellae _____   **5.** amīcae _____   **8.** vīllae _____

3. Flāvia et Aurēlia _____   **6.** pictūra _____   **9.** Cornēlia _____

Activity 2g Singular and Plural Verbs

In the story on page 7 of your textbook, find all the verbs that end in **-t** *and* **-nt** *and copy them in the spaces below. Do not copy the same word more than once.*

-t	-nt
1. _____	7. _____
2. _____	8. _____
3. _____	9. _____
4. _____	10. _____
5. _____
6. _____

Look at how these verbs were used in the story. Then complete the following sentences:

1. When the subject of a Latin sentence is plural, the verb ends in _____.

2. When the subject of a Latin sentence is singular, the verb ends in _____.

Activity 2h Singular and Plural Subjects and Verbs

Underline each subject. Then circle the verbs that complete the sentences correctly:

Cornēlia sub arbore (sedet / sedent). Flāvia in agrīs (currit / currunt). Puellae (est / sunt) amīcae. Iam puellae ad vīllam (currit / currunt) et in vīllā (sedet / sedent). Cornēlia (est / sunt) laeta quod amīca eius in vīllā vīcīnā aestāte (habitat / habitant).

Applying What You Have Learned

Activity 2i Writing the Language

Translate the following English sentences into Latin. Include all long marks. Use the stories and vocabulary lists in your textbook, as well as the vocabulary lists in this book, to help you:

1. In the picture there are girls, named Cornelia and Flavia.

   _____

2. Cornelia is happy because (she)* sits under a tree and reads.

   _____

3. Flavia is a friend who lives in a neighboring country house.

   _____

4. Flavia is running in the fields.

   _____

5. In a short time the girls walk out of the fields.

   _____

*Do not translate *she* with a separate word.

Activity 2j Expanding Your English Vocabulary

For each italicized English word below, give the related Latin word and below it the meaning of that Latin word. Then complete each sentence by filling in a word at the right:

Latin Word
Meaning of the Latin Word   **If you ...**

1. _____   behave in an *amicable* manner,
                                 your actions are
   _____   _____

2. _____   are employed in *agriculture*, you
                                 work a lot in the
   _____   _____

3. _____ are an *ambulatory* patient in a hospital, you are able to _____

_____

4. _____ are amazed by the *brevity* of a speech, you are amazed by its _____

_____

5. _____ report on *current* events, you are reporting on events that are presently _____

_____

6. _____ work at a *temporary* job, you are working for a limited _____

_____

7. (two words) _____ *subscribe* to a magazine, you _____ your name _____

_____

_____ _____ an agreement to pay for regular delivery of the magazine. _____

_____

8. _____ work *strenuously*, you are working with a lot of _____

_____

9. _____ pay a *nominal* fee, you are paying an amount so small that it is a fee in _____ only. _____

_____

10. _____ have *amiable* companions, you expect them to be _____

_____

Activity 2k Reading Latin

Look at the new vocabulary beneath this story. Then read the story, noting singular and plural subjects, verbs, and complements. Reread the story for comprehension. Then answer the questions below with complete Latin sentences:

Girls in the Fields I

Ecce! Sunt puellae in agrīs. Puellae sunt Flāvia et Cornēlia. Flāvia et Cornēlia sunt amīcae et in agrīs saepe ambulant. Sed hodiē Cornēlia currit. Brevī tempore etiam Flāvia currit. Cūr puellae currunt? Currunt quod sunt vaccae quoque in agrīs. Vaccae lentē ambulant, sed vaccae sunt magnae et puellae sunt parvae. Puellae ex agrīs currunt quod timidae sunt.

vaccae, *cows*   **magnae,** *large, big*   **parvae,** *small*   **timidae,** *afraid, fearful, timid*

1. Quae sunt in agrīs?   **Quae…?** *Who (pl.)…? What (pl.)…?*

_____

2. Quae hodiē currunt?

_____

3. Quae magnae sunt?

_____

4. Quid faciunt puellae?

_____

5. Cūr puellae ex agrīs currunt?

_____

IN THE GARDEN

> *In addition to vocabulary and the story, the activities in this chapter focus on:*
> 1. the singular and plural of nouns and adjectives ending in *-a* in the singular.
> 2. the singular and plural of nouns and adjectives ending in *-us* in the singular and of the nouns **puer** and **vir**.
> 3. singular and plural forms of verbs.
> 4. subjects and parts of speech.

Vocabulary

Activity 3a Vocabulary

Study the vocabulary list on pages 206–207 alone or with a partner. Note that we give singular and plural forms of nouns, adjectives, and verbs and that we divide nouns and verbs into groups.

The Story

Activity 3b Comprehension

Use the story in Chapter 3 of your textbook to determine if these statements are true (T) or false (F). If the statement is false, write a correct statement below it:

1. Dāvus est vir Rōmānus.   T   F

_____

2. Dāvus est īrātus quod puerī clāmant.   T   F

_____

3. Mārcus et Sextus in piscīnam cadunt.   T   F

_____

4. Puerī ex hortō currunt.   T   F

_____

5. Dāvus gemit quod dēfessus est.   T   F

_____

6. Mārcus est īrātus quod statua est in piscīnā.　　　　　　T　　F

_____

7. Mārcus et Sextus rīdent quod Dāvus in piscīnam cadit.　　T　　F

_____

Forms

Nouns and Adjectives: Singular and Plural

Activity 3c Singulars and Plurals

Make each sentence plural. Change all subjects, verbs, and adjectives. The first one is done for you:

1. Puella rīdet.　　　　　　_____*Puellae rīdent.*_____

2. Servus labōrat.　　　　　_____

3. Puer est laetus.　　　　　_____

4. Puella est īrāta.　　　　　_____

5. Vir clāmat.　　　　　　　_____

Make each sentence singular. Change all subjects, verbs, and adjectives:

6. Puellae clāmant.　　　　　_____

7. Servī ambulant.　　　　　_____

8. Puellae sunt strēnuae.　　_____

9. Puerī sunt strēnuī.　　　　_____

10. Virī rīdent.　　　　　　　_____

Activity 3d Endings of Nouns, Adjectives, and Verbs

Decide whether the incomplete words are nouns, adjectives, or verbs and whether they should be singular or plural. Then fill in the correct endings to complete the meaning of each sentence:

Dum Cornēlia et **Flāvia**, puellae Rōmān_____, in agrīs **lentē** ambulant, **Mārcus**

et **Sextus**, puerī Rōmān_____, in hortō clāma_____ et rīde_____. **Neque** puerī

Rōmān_____ **neque** puellae Rōmān_____ in agrīs labōrant, **sed** serv_____ in agrīs et

vīllīs labōrant. **Servus** gemit **quod** dēfess_____ **est,** sed puell_____ nōn gemunt

14 CHAPTER 3

quod **laetae sunt.** Puer_____ nōn **sunt dēfessī** quod nōn labōra_____. **Flāvia** nōn **est**

dēfess_____ quod **est** puell_____ strēnua.

neque … neque … , *neither … nor …*

Now, study the words in bold type in the preceding story. Put an S over each subject, the letters LV over each linking verb, and a C over each complement. Then put a V over all other verbs. Finally, put the letters ADV over each adverb and CONJ over each conjunction.

Applying What You Have Learned

Activity 3e Writing the Language

Translate the following English sentences into Latin. Include all long marks. Use the stories and vocabulary lists in your textbook, as well as the vocabulary lists in this book, to help you:

1. Slaves work in the country house and farm.

   _____

2. Davus works because he is a slave.

   _____

3. The Roman girls live in the same country house.

   _____

4. The boys do not work but run in the garden.

   _____

5. The men are now sitting in the country house because they are reading and writing.

   _____

Activity 3f Expanding Your English Vocabulary

Using the word bank below, write the word that could replace the italicized word or words in each sentence or could complete the sentence. Use the Latin words in parentheses to help determine the meaning of the English words. Then write the English translation of each Latin word in the word bank:

1. Davus usually tends to the *gardening*. _____

2. The boys' loud *shouting* annoys Davus. _____

3. The boys often play *childish* pranks. _____

4. The boys often *laugh at* each other. _____

5. Davus watches and slowly becomes quite *angry*. _____

6. Davus often performs tasks requiring much work;

   these tasks are _____. _____

7. Davus enjoys working alone; he likes _____ work. _____

8. Davus's age has not diminished his *manly* strength. _____

9. Davus cannot endure the boy's *laughable* antics. _____

10. Marcus recognizes the slow *foot-fall* of Davus's walk. _____

laborious (**labōrant**) _____	horticulture (**hortō**) _____
cadence (**cadit**) _____	ridiculous (**rīdent**) _____
clamor (**clāmant**) _____	puerile (**puer**) _____
deride (**rīdent**) _____	irate (**īrātus**) _____
solitary (**sōlus**) _____	virile (**vir**) _____

Activity 3g Reading Latin

Look at the new vocabulary beneath this story. Then read the story, noting whether subjects,
adjectives, and verbs are singular or plural. Reread the story for comprehension. Then answer
the questions below with complete Latin sentences:

Boys and Girls in the Fields

Puerī et puellae in agrīs sunt. Cornēlia dēfessa sedet et Flāvia sōla ambulat.
Puerī laetī sunt. Clāmant et rīdent. Hodiē Mārcus est strēnuus et in agrīs currit.
Sextus in mūrō stat. Mūrus est magnus, sed Sextus nōn timet.

Etiam in agrīs sunt multae vaccae et magnus taurus. Cornēlia nōn timet.
"Ecce!" clāmat. "Est magnus taurus."

Flāvia est puella timida. Flāvia aufugit quod taurus est magnus. Brevī
tempore Mārcus et Cornēlia quoque ex agrīs currunt. Sed quid Sextus facit?
Sextus sōlus nōn aufugit quod nōn timet. Puer in magnō mūrō stat.

in mūrō, *on a wall*   **taurus,** *(a/the) bull*

stat, *(he/she) stands, is standing*   **timida,** *afraid, fearful, timid*

magnus, *large, big*   **aufugit,** *(he/she) runs away*

timet, *(he/she) is afraid*

vaccac, *cows*

1. Quī laetī sunt?   **Quī...?** *Who...?* (pl.)

_____

2. Quis in agrīs currit?

_____

3. Quis est timida?

_____

4. Quis est magnus?

_____

5. Quī ex agrīs currunt?

_____

A MISCHIEF-MAKER

In addition to vocabulary and the story, the activities in this chapter focus on:
1. direct objects, including **mē** and **tē**.
2. producing direct object forms of nouns.
3. the core elements of Latin sentences with intransitive, transitive, and linking verbs.

Vocabulary

Activity 4a Vocabulary

Study the vocabulary list on pages 208–209 alone or with a partner. Note that we now list personal pronouns separately. Note also that we now list the singular direct object forms of nouns and adjectives. Go to the corresponding list on the Companion website where you will find an additional list of subject and direct object forms of nouns that you have met so far.

The Story

Activity 4b Vocabulary in Context

Fill in the blanks in the following sentences with Latin words to match the English cues:

1. Sextus Cornēliam _____ _____. (always) (annoys)

2. Sextus puer _____ est. (troublesome, annoying)

3. Cornēlia sub arbore _____. (sleeps)

4. Sextus _____ _____. (stealthily) (approaches)

5. Sextus Cornēliam _____ _____. (does not like)

6. Arborem _____ _____. (therefore) (he climbs)

7. Subitō _____ _____ clāmat. (in a loud voice)

8. _____ est _____. (The branch) (weak)

9. Mārcus Sextum _____. (catches sight of)

10. Mārcus clāmat, "_____, _____!" (Come down, Sextus!)

11. Sextus clāmat, "Nihil _____ _____!" (frightens me)

12. Cornēlia _____ clāmat, "_____, Sexte!" (anxious, worried) (Be careful!)

13. Sed Sextus nihil _____. (hears)

14. Nihil quoque _____ Sextus. (sees)

15. _____ Sextus ex arbore cadit. (Then)

16. _____ Cornēliam _____. (The crash) (frightens)

17. Cornēlia clāmat, "Nihil _____ _____!" (frightens you)

Building the Meaning

Direct Objects and the Ending *-m*

Activity 4c Identifying Direct Objects

Find and copy seven different nouns that serve as direct objects of verbs in the story on page 19 of your textbook:

1. _____   **3.** _____   **5.** _____   **7.** _____

2. _____   **4.** _____   **6.** _____

Activity 4d Identifying Subjects and Direct Objects

Write S next to the forms in the following list that could serve as subjects and DO next to the forms that could serve as direct objects:

1. puellam _____   **8.** vōx _____   **15.** tē _____

2. Mārcus _____   **9.** rāmus _____   **16.** arborem _____

3. fragōrem _____   **10.** vōcem _____   **17.** Sextum _____

4. puer _____   **11.** amīcam _____   **18.** Cornēlia _____

5. mē _____   **12.** virum _____   **19.** rāmum _____

6. puerum _____   **13.** fragor _____   **20.** arbor _____

7. Mārcum _____   **14.** vir _____   **21.** Cornēliam _____

Activity 4e Forming Direct Objects

Give the direct object forms of the following nouns:

1. vir   _____

2. arbor   _____

3. Cornēlia   _____

4. servus   _____

5. amīca   _____

6. puella   _____

7. vōx   _____

8. puer   _____

9. Mārcus   _____

10. fragor   _____

Activity 4f Noun Endings

Fill in the endings of the nouns in the following story, according to the function of each noun in its sentence:

Dum Cornēli_____ dormit, Sext_____ arbor_____ ascendit. Cornēlia Sext_____

nōn videt, quod dormit. Mārc_____ ad arborem currit et fragōr_____ audit quod

Sext_____ ex arbore cadit. Cornēli_____ nōn iam dormit. Mārcus et Cornēlia

Sext_____ cōnspiciunt et rīdent. Sextus Cornēli_____ et Mārc_____ nōn iam amat.

Core Elements of Latin Sentences

Activity 4g Identifying Core Elements of Latin Sentences

Read the story below, and study the words and phrases in bold type (phrases are underlined). Put an S over subjects, the letters IV over intransitive verbs, TV over transitive verbs, and DO over direct objects. Also, put LV over linking verbs and C over complements:

> **Sextus** est <u>**puer molestus**</u>. **Cornēlia** igitur **Sextum** nōn **amat**. Hodiē sub
>
> arbore **dormit Cornēlia**. **Sextus puellam cōnspicit** et fūrtim **appropinquat**.
>
> **Arborem ascendit** et subitō magnā vōce **clāmat**. **Vōcem Cornēlia audit** sed
>
> **Sextum** nōn **videt**. <u>**Magna vōx**</u> **Cornēliam terret**.

Applying What You Have Learned

Activity 4h Writing the Language

Translate the following English sentences into Latin. Remember that the direct object usually appears in front of the verb in Latin. Include all long marks. Use the stories and vocabulary lists in your textbook, as well as the vocabulary lists in this book, to help you:

1. Today Sextus climbs the tree.

_____

2. Sextus frightens Cornelia while Cornelia sleeps under the tree.

_____

3. Marcus sees the weak branch and then approaches.

_____

4. Cornelia laughs because Sextus falls out of the tree, but Sextus groans.

_____

5. Sextus no longer climbs the tree.

_____

Activity 4i Expanding Your English Vocabulary

For each italicized English word below, give the related Latin word and below it the meaning of that Latin word. Then complete each sentence by filling in a word at the right:

Latin Word
Meaning of the Latin Word   **If you …**

1. _____   live in a *dormitory*, you live in a building
   _____   designed for   _____

2. _____   have lost the *video* portion of a broadcast,
   _____   you have lost the portion intended to be _____

3. _____   are a judge at a musical *audition*,
   _____   you must give each performer a careful _____

4. _____   are sent to an *infirmary*, you are sent to a
   _____   place for the treatment of those who are _____

5. _____   *terrify* children with your Halloween
   _____   costume, you are _____ them.   _____

6. _____   are an *amateur* athlete, you take part in
   _____   a sport because you _____ it.   _____

7. _____   *ascend* the stairs, you _____ them.   _____
   _____

8. _____   are *descending* in an elevator, you are _____
   _____

9. _____   wear a *conspicuous* color, you wear a color
   _____   that is easy to _____ in a crowd.   _____

10. _____   give a *furtive* glance, you look at someone
    _____   in a _____ manner.   _____

Activity 4j Reading Latin

*Look at the new vocabulary beneath this story. Then read the story, using your knowledge of the new noun endings to distinguish direct objects from subjects. Reread the story for comprehension. Then mark whether each statement below the story is V = **Vērum** (True) or F = **Falsum** (False):*

Girls in the Fields II

Cornēlia et Flāvia in agrīs ad vīllam ambulant.

Cornēlia, "Sextus est puer molestus," clāmat. "Semper mē vexat. Semper currit et clāmat et arborem ascendit."

"Ita vērō!" inquit Flāvia. "Sextus mē quoque vexat et terret. Nihil Sextum terret. Ubi est Mārcus hodiē? Mārcus mē nōn vexat."

Cornēlia, "Mārcus quoque," inquit, "molestus est! Puerī saepe in hortō currunt et in agrīs arborem ascendunt. Ecce! Sextus arborem iam ascendit." Subitō puellae magnum fragōrem audiunt. Sextus ē rāmō īnfirmō cadit. Mārcus eum cōnspicit et magnā vōce rīdet. Flāvia et Cornēlia quoque Sextum cōnspiciunt et rīdent quod puerum molestum nōn amant. Tum Mārcum videt Flāvia et rīdet quod Mārcum amat.

Ubi...? *Where...?*	**eum,** *him*		
1. Sextus Cornēliam semper vexat.		V	F
2. Flāvia quoque Sextum vexat et terret.		V	F
3. Mārcus Flāviam vexat.		V	F
4. Flāvia Sextum nōn amat.		V	F
5. Mārcus Flāviam videt et rīdet.		V	F

MARCUS TO THE RESCUE

> *In addition to vocabulary and the story, the activities in this chapter focus on:*
> 1. complementary infinitives.
> 2. verbs that may be used with infinitives to complete their meaning.

Vocabulary

Activity 5a Vocabulary

Study the vocabulary list on pages 210–211 alone or with a partner. Go to the corresponding list on the Companion website where you will find a list of verbs used with complementary infinitives and the infinitives of all verbs met so far.

The Story

Activity 5b Vocabulary in Context

Fill in the blanks with Latin words to match the English cues:

1. Mārcus nōn est _____. (cowardly)

2. Sextus est _____. (rash)

3. _____ Cornēlia _____ Flāvia est in vīllā. (Neither) (nor)

4. Puellae _____ rīvum sedent. (near)

5. _____ est _____. (The day) (warm)

6. Sed _____ est _____. (the stream) (cool)

7. Puellae _____ _____ currunt. (into the woods)

8. Dum puellae _____, _____ ad rīvum dēscendit. (wander) (a wolf)

9. Lupus puellās terrēre _____ _____. (does not want)

10. Sed puellae sunt _____. (frightened)

11. Puellae clāmant, "_____
    _____!" ("Help!")

12. Sextus et Mārcus _____ _____ currunt. (toward the girls)

13. Puellae _____ vident. (them)

14. Mārcus rāmum _____. (grabs hold of)

15. Mārcus lupum repellere _____ _____. (is not afraid)

16. Statim Mārcus lupum _____. (drives off)

17. Puellae currunt et ad vīllam _____. (arrive)

18. Cornēlius et Aurēlia eās _____. (welcome)

19. Puellae _____ sunt. (safe)

Building the Meaning

Activity 5c The Complementary Infinitive

Complete the following sentence:

Infinitives in Latin end with the letters _____ and are translated into English with the word _____.

Keeping to the sense of the story in your textbook, complete the following Latin sentences with infinitives from the word bank. You may use a word more than once, and there are more infinitives in the word bank than you will need. Then translate each sentence:

1. Cornēlia in silvā _____ vult.

_____

2. Mārcus arborem _____ nōn vult.

_____

3. Sextum nihil _____ potest.

_____

4. Sextus, ubi lupus appropinquat, arborem _____ vult.

_____

5. Mārcus lupum _____ potest.

_____

6. Sextus ex arbore _____ timet.

_____

| repellere   ascendere   respondēre   dēscendere   arripere   ambulāre   terrēre   excipere |

Activity 5d Completing Sentences with Correct Verb Forms

Read each sentence. Decide whether the subject needs a singular or plural verb or whether a complementary infinitive is needed. Circle the word that correctly completes the sentence. Then answer the questions below in complete English sentences:

Mārcus et Sextus in silvam (ambulant / ambulat). Sextus (clāmat / clāmant), "Ego arborem (ascendit / ascendere) volō." Sed Mārcus arborem (dēscendere / ascendere) nōn vult. Tum Sextus, "Tū es ignāvus." Statim Sextus arborem (ascendit / ascendere). Lupus venit sed Sextum (terret / terrēre) nōn potest, quod puer est in arbore. Mārcus nōn est perterritus et lupum (repellere / repellit). Sextus (dēscendit / dēscendere) nōn vult quod est ignāvus.

es, *(you) are*   **venit,** *(it) comes*

1. What does Sextus want to do?

_____

2. Why does Sextus call Marcus cowardly?

_____

3. Is the wolf able to frighten Sextus? Explain why or why not.

_____

4. Is Marcus frightened?

_____

5. How does Marcus respond?

_____

6. Where is Sextus at the end of the story and why?

_____

Activity 5e Verbs with Complementary Infinitives

Circle four verbs that can be used with complementary infinitives and give their meanings:

1. ambulat = _____   4. repellit = _____

2. terret = _____   5. currit = _____

3. timet = _____   6. potest = _____

7. clāmat = _____   **9.** vult = _____

8. audit = _____   **10.** parat = _____

Applying What You Have Learned

Activity 5f Writing the Language

Translate the following English sentences into Latin. Include all long marks. Use the stories and vocabulary lists in your textbook, as well as the vocabulary lists in this book, to help you:

1. Sextus is an energetic boy who always wants to climb a tree.

_____

2. When a wolf approaches, Sextus immediately runs into the woods and seeks a tree.

_____

3. He* is not able to climb the tree.

_____

4. He* grabs hold of a branch and drives off the wolf.

_____

5. At last he* runs out of the woods and arrives safe(ly) at the farmhouse.

_____

*Do not translate *he* with a separate word.

Activity 5g Expanding Your English Vocabulary

Using the word bank on the next page, write the word that could replace the italicized word or words in each sentence. Use the Latin words in parentheses to help determine the meaning of the English words. Then write the English translation of each Latin word in the word bank:

1. The Roman army recruited *helping* troops from the provinces.   _____

2. In the heat of the summer, the children often seek the *extremely cold* water of the stream.   _____

3. When you make a *mistake*, you "wander" from what is correct.   _____

4. Marcus's quick action provided *safety* for the girls.   _____

5. With the *arrival* of summer, the girls like to walk in the fields.   _____

6. Sextus often gets into difficulty because of his *recklessness*.   _____

7. The wolf left a *wandering* trail through the forest.   _____

8. The girls chose this tree because of its *nearness* to the stream.   _____

9. Sextus is too *afraid* to climb down from the tree.   _____

10. Marcus's actions *drove* the wolf *off*.   _____

temerity (**temerārius**) _____	repelled (**repellit**) _____
propinquity (**prope**) _____	erratic (**errant**) _____
auxiliary (**auxilium**) _____	frigid (**frīgidus**) _____
timid (**timet**) _____	advent (**adveniunt**) _____
error (**errant**) _____	salvation (**salvae**) _____

Activity 5h Reading Latin

Look at the new vocabulary on the next page. Then read the story, noting infinitives and endings that mark direct objects. Reread the story for comprehension. Then answer the questions with complete Latin sentences:

Serves Him Right

Hodiē Mārcus in agrīs lūdit quod canem habet. Canis in agrīs laetus lūdit. Brevī tempore Sextus ad Mārcum currit. Puerī et canis iam in agrīs lūdunt. Clāmor est magnus!

Ecce! Cornēlia et Flāvia in agrīs prope canem errant. Flāvia fēlem habet. Canis fēlem videt et magnā vōce lātrat. Fēlēs canem timet et aufugit. Est in agrīs magna arbor. Fēlēs arborem petit et ascendit dum canis lātrat.

Flāvia est perterrita quod fēlēs ex arbore dēscendere nōn potest. Flāvia arborem ascendere timet. Sextus, quī est puer temerārius, rīdet et clāmat, "Flāvia arborem ascendere nōn vult! Puellae semper sunt ignāvae!" Sextus arborem statim ascendit quod fēlem petere parat. Fēlēs subitō ex arbore cadit et aufugit. Flāvia fēlem salvam excipit. Sextus ex arbore dēscendere nōn potest quod tunica in rāmīs haeret.

lūdit, *(he/she) plays*	**lātrat,** *(he/she) barks*
canis, *dog*	**aufugit,** *(he/she) runs away*
habet, *(he/she) has*	**haeret,** *is stuck*
fēlēs, *cat*	

1. Quid fēlēs facere nōn potest?

_____

2. Quid Flāvia facere timet?

_____

3. Quid Sextus facere parat?

_____

4. Quid Sextus facere nōn potest?

_____

EARLY IN THE DAY

In addition to vocabulary and the story, the activities in this chapter focus on:
1. the phrase **necesse est** and its infinitive.
2. identifying nouns you have met as masculine or feminine in gender.
3. using correct endings on adjectives in sentences.
4. identifying the gender of nouns in noun-adjective pairs.

Vocabulary

Activity 6a Vocabulary

Study the vocabulary list on pages 212–213 alone or with a partner. Go to the corresponding list on the Companion website where you will find a list of nouns that do not end in -a or -us with their genders and direct object forms.

The Story

Activity 6b Dictation and Vocabulary

Fill in the blanks as your teacher reads the story aloud. Then go back and write the meanings of the Latin words in the spaces provided. As you do so, add pronouns as subjects for any verbs that do not have expressed subjects in the Latin:

1. _____ = _____ **2.** _____ =

_____, sed Cornēlia **3.** _____ = _____

et **4.** _____ = _____ vīllam ambulat. Adhūc dormiunt

5. _____ = _____ et **6.** _____ =

_____ et Mārcus. **7.** _____ = _____ Sextus

dormit **8.** _____ = _____Cornēliam vexat. Nōn

9. _____ = _____ dormiunt servī et ancillae.

10. _____ = _____ iam surgunt et labōrāre parant

quod Cornēlium et Aurēliam timent.

Cornēlia ancillam, nōmine Syram, **11.** _____ = _____

quae vīllam **12.** _____ = _____ et alteram,

nōmine Thressam, quae **13.** _____ = _____

14. _____ = _____ parat. Multī servī

15. _____ = _____ in agrōs currunt ubi

16. _____ = _____ labōrant. **17.** _____ =

_____ ē rīvō in vīllam **18.** _____ = _____.

    Iam **19.** _____ = _____ Cornēlius et Aurēlia. Cornēlius

petit Dāvum quī in hortō est. Īrātus subitō est Cornēlius. Dāvum **20.** _____

= _____ quod sub arbore sedet neque labōrat. Dāvus, ubi Cornēlium audit,

statim **21.** _____ = _____ et labōrāre parat.

    Aurēlia Cornēliam **22.** _____ = _____ vīllam

23. _____ = _____. Ancillae vīllam

24. _____ = _____, cibum coquunt,

25. _____ _____ = _____. Reprehendit

Aurēlia ancillās sī ignāvae sunt. Mātrem observat Cornēlia et **26.** _____

_____ = _____ māter facit facere parat. Mātrem

27. _____ = _____ vult, sed ipsa neque servum neque

ancillam reprehendit. Servī et ancillae **28.** _____ = _____

strēnuē labōrant. **29.** _____ = _____ neque servum neque

ancillam **30.** _____ = _____.

Building the Meaning

Infinitive with Impersonal Verbal Phrase

Activity 6c Translating *necesse est* and Its Infinitive

The following is a list of chores that need to be completed. Circle the infinitive in each sentence and translate the sentence into English:

  1. Necesse est vīllam pūrgāre.

  _____

  2. Necesse est Aurēliam adiuvāre.

  _____

3. Necesse est aquam ē rīvō in vīllam portāre.

_____

4. Necesse est cibum coquere.

_____

5. Necesse est in agrīs strēnuē labōrāre.

_____

Nouns and Adjectives: Gender

Activity 6d Gender of Nouns

*Give the gender of the following nouns. Write **M** for masculine and **F** for feminine:*

1. pictūra _____ **3.** clāmor _____ **5.** pater _____ **7.** vōx _____ **9.** fragor _____

2. lupus _____ **4.** vīlla _____ **6.** rīvus _____ **8.** arbor _____ **10.** māter _____

Activity 6e Nouns and Adjectives

*In the following sentences, write **N** over each noun and **ADJ** over each adjective. Then draw arrows from adjectives to the nouns they describe. Finally, give the gender of the underlined noun:*

1. Dāvus semper est sollicitus. Gender: _____

2. Multae arborēs in agrīs sunt. Gender: _____

3. Sextus magnam arborem ascendit. Gender: _____

4. Puellae dēfessae iam dormiunt. Gender: _____

5. Rāmī sunt īnfirmī. Gender: _____

6. Sextus ignāvus nōn est. Gender: _____

7. Puerum laetum nihil terret. Gender: _____

8. Sextus ex arbore cadit et magnum fragōrem facit. Gender: _____

9. Puellae magnam vōcem audiunt. Gender: _____

10. <u>Puellae</u> sollicitae sunt et ad Sextum currunt. Gender: _____

11. <u>Sextus</u> est salvus. Gender: _____

12. <u>Aqua</u> est calida. Gender: _____

13. Necesse est <u>cibum</u> frīgidum coquere. Gender: _____

14. <u>Pater</u> in vīllā scrībit sollicitus. Gender: _____

15. Cornēlia <u>mātrem</u> in vīllā cōnspicit sollicitam. Gender: _____

Activity 6f Adjective Agreement

In each sentence, write the correct ending on the adjective so that it modifies the underlined noun. Be sure to note the gender, case, and number of the underlined noun. Then translate the sentence:

1. Mārcus <u>togam</u> praetext_____ petit.

   _____

2. <u>Puellae</u> dēfess_____ ad vīllam ambulant.

   _____

3. Magn_____ <u>vōcēs</u> puerōs terrent.

   _____

4. <u>Puerī</u> strēnu_____ in agrīs currunt.

   _____

5. Audit Cornēlius magn_____ <u>clāmōrem</u>.

   _____

6. Sextus magn_____ <u>arborem</u> ascendit.

   _____

7. Audiunt Mārcus et Cornēlia magn_____ <u>fragōrem</u>.

   _____

8. Puer <u>mātrem</u> laet_____ videt.

   _____

9. <u>Pater</u> sollicit_____ dormīre nōn potest.

_____

10. Cornēlia magn_____ <u>vōcem</u> audit.

_____

Activity 6g Gender of Nouns

Using the adjectives as evidence, give the gender of the nouns in the following noun-adjective pairs:

1. canis magnus _____   3. iānitor sēmisomnus _____   5. aestās calida _____

2. nox longa _____   4. urbs magna _____   6. diēs longus _____

Applying What You Have Learned

Activity 6h Writing the Language

Translate the following English sentences into Latin. Include all long marks. Use the stories and vocabulary lists in your textbook, as well as the vocabulary lists in this book, to help you:

1. It is not yet light, but the Roman girl rises.

_____

2. Marcus and Sextus, the annoying boys, are still sleeping.

_____

3. Many slave-women work hard, when the mother is angry.

_____

4. Davus is angry because the slaves are lazy.

_____

5. Cornelius is happy because many slaves and many slave-women work hard and take care of the big country house and farm.

_____

_____

Activity 6i Expanding Your English Vocabulary

*For each italicized English word below, give the related Latin word and below it the meaning
of that Latin word. Then complete each sentence by filling in a word at the right:*

**Latin Word
Meaning of the Latin Word**

If you . . .

1. _____

   _____

   have *aquatic* plants, you have plants
   that grow in   _____

2. _____

   _____

   are an *observant* witness, you are good
   at _____ all the details.   _____

3. _____

   _____

   commit a *reprehensible* act, you do
   something that is   _____

4. _____

   _____

   watch the waves *surging*, you watch
   the waves as they   _____

5. _____

   _____

   look through a *translucent* curtain,
   you can see only _____ through it.   _____

6. _____

   _____

   have *maternal* feelings, you are feeling
   like a   _____

7. _____

   _____

   have a *docile* pet, your pet is easy to   _____

8. _____

   _____

   are determining the *paternity* of a child,
   you are looking for the identity of the   _____

9. _____

   _____

   are fighting an *insurgent* population,
   you are fighting a population that is   _____

10. _____

    _____

    employ *ancillary* staff, you employ staff
    members who provide extra   _____

Activity 6j Reading Latin

Look at the new vocabulary beneath this story. Then read the story, noting noun-adjective pairs and infinitives. Reread the story for comprehension. Then rewrite the sentences below the story so that they are correct:

Davus Is Tired

Nōndum lūcet, sed Dāvus et aliī servī et ancillae iam surgunt. Brevī tempore ancillae cibum coquere et magnam vīllam cūrāre parant. Multī servī ē vīllā ad agrōs ambulant ubi strēnuē labōrāre parant. In agrīs sunt magnī bovēs et multae ovēs. Aliī servī aquam in vīllam portant. Dāvus tamen in agrīs nōn labōrat quod hortum purgāre necesse est. Dāvus in hortum ambulat et gemit quod statua adhūc in piscīnā est. Necesse est strēnuē labōrāre.

Dāvus nōn sedet quod Aurēliam et Cornēlium timet. Piscīnam pūrgāre parat, sed mox sedet quod est dēfessus. Audit Aurēliam, quae prope hortum est. Aurēlia Dāvum ignāvum cōnspicit. "Cavē, Dāve," Aurēlia īrāta clāmat. "Tempus est labōrāre!"

Subitō Dāvus Cornēlium audit, quī in vīllā clāmat, "Ubi est Dāvus? Dormitne?" Dāvus gemit et surgit quod Cornēlium īrātum timet.

aliī, *other*　　**bovēs,** *oxen*　　**ovēs,** *sheep*

1. Magnae ancillae vīllam cūrāre parant.

_____

2. Ad agrōs multōs servī ē vīllā ambulant.

_____

3. Multī ovēs et magnae bovēs in agrīs sunt.

_____

4. Dāvum ignāva Aurēlia cōnspicit.

_____

5. Cornēlium īrātus Dāvus timet.

_____

NEWS FROM ROME

> *In addition to vocabulary and the story, the activities in this chapter focus on:*
> 1. nominative and accusative plural forms of nouns.
> 2. singular and plural subjects and direct objects.
> 3. identifying the declension of a noun.
> 4. translating sentences with subjects, verbs, and direct objects in any order.
> 5. determining whether nouns ending in *-ēs* are nominative or accusative plural when met in sentences.

Vocabulary

Activity 7a Vocabulary

Study the vocabulary list on pages 214–215 alone or with a partner. Note that we now give both the accusative singular and plural forms of nouns and adjectives. Go to the corresponding list on the Companion website where you will find an additional list of all 3rd declension nouns that you have met so far with their genders.

The Story

Activity 7b Questions on the Story

Write the name of the correct character from the story in your textbook to complete the answers to the following questions:

1. Quis multās epistulās scrībere vult? _____ multās epistulās scrībere vult.

2. Quis puerōs salūtat? _____ puerōs salūtat.

3. Quis Gāium Cornēlium petit? _____ Gāium Cornēlium petit.

4. Quis nūntium in vīllam dūcit? _____ nūntium in vīllam dūcit.

5. Quis epistulam trādit? _____ epistulam trādit.

6. Quis epistulam legit? _____ epistulam legit.

7. Quis "Ēheu!" inquit? _____ "Ēheu!" inquit.

8. Quis senātōrēs revocat? _____ senātōrēs revocat.

9. Quis est laetus quod necesse est Rōmam īre? _____ est laetus quod necesse est Rōmam īre.

10. Quis ad urbem īre nōn potest? _____ ad urbem īre nōn potest.

Forms

Nouns and Adjectives: The Endings *-ās*, *-ōs*, and *-ēs*

Activity 7c Nominative and Accusative Plural Forms of Nouns

Fill in the nominative and accusative plural endings on the following nouns according to their declension:

Nom.	Acc.		Nom.	Acc.		Nom.	Acc.
1. vōc_____	vōc_____		3. puer_____	puer_____		5. patr_____	patr_____
2. serv_____	serv_____		4. agr_____	agr_____		6. puell_____	puell_____

Activity 7d Subjects and Direct Objects

Fill in each blank with the correct nominative or accusative form of the noun in parentheses. Fill in a singular or plural form as directed. Be sure to note the declension of each noun you fill in before you decide what ending it should have. Remember that the nominative case is used for the subject and the accusative case is used for the direct object.

1. Cornēlius _____ scrībit. (epistula: sing.)

2. Nūntius _____ salūtat. (puer: pl.)

3. _____ Dāvum saepe vexant. (puer: pl.)

4. Dāvus multās _____ audit. (vōx: pl.)

5. _____ rīvum cōnspiciunt. (puella: pl.)

6. Cornēlia _____ audit. (vōx: sing.)

7. Multae _____ Cornēliam terrent. (vōx: pl.)

8. _____ Dāvus reprehendit. (servus: pl.)

9. Puerī _____ sollicitōs in viā vident. (pater: pl.)

10. Puerōs sollicitōs _____ in viā vident. (pater: pl.)

11. Lupus _____ terret. (puella: pl.)

12. _____ puellam sollicitam vident. (servus: pl.)

13. Mārcus _____ petit. (pater: sing.)

14. Servī _____ cōnspiciunt. (ager: sing.)

15. Dāvus _____ spectat. (ager: pl.)

Building the Meaning

Reading with Attention to Cases

Activity 7e Reading with Attention to Cases

Identify words in the nominative and accusative case and determine which are subjects and which are direct objects. Underline the subjects and circle the direct objects. Then translate the sentences:

1. Nūntium puerī et puella in agrīs vīcīnīs cōnspiciunt.

_____

2. Ubi puerōs nūntius salūtat, Cornēlia ad vīllam currit.

_____

3. Mātrem Cornēlia statim petit.

_____

4. "Nūntium," inquit Cornēlia, "puerī in agrīs nunc salūtant."

_____

5. "Necesse est," respondet Aurēlia, "cibum parāre."

_____

6. Cibum ancillae parant.

_____

7. Cornēlius, ubi advenit nūntius, eum salūtat.

_____

8. Epistulam Cornēlius legit.

_____

9. Aurēlia nūntium salūtat et "Ecce! Cibum ancilla," inquit, "portat."

_____

10. Statim advenit ancilla, et cibum portat.

_____

Nominative or Accusative Plural?
How Do You Decide?

Activity 7f Nominative or Accusative?

Read each of the following sentences and circle the case of the underlined noun. Then explain why you decided it must be that case:

1. Flāvia <u>arborēs</u> cōnspicit.

   NOM.   ACC.   reason: _____

   _____

2. Hodiē Flāvia <u>arborēs</u> ascendere vult.

   NOM.   ACC.   reason: _____

   _____

3. Quod <u>arborēs</u> Sextum nunc terrent, puer molestus ad vīllam redit.

   NOM.   ACC.   reason: _____

   _____

4. Brevī tempore <u>mātrēs</u> puellās revocant.

   NOM.   ACC.   reason: _____

   _____

5. Puellae <u>vocēs</u> nōn audiunt.

   NOM.   ACC.   reason: _____

   _____

6. Aurēlia, "Ēheu!" inquit, "puellae <u>arborēs</u> nōn ascendunt."

   NOM.   ACC.   reason: _____

   _____

7. <u>Mātrēs</u> puellās ex arbore dēscendere iubent.

   NOM.   ACC.   reason: _____

   _____

Applying What You Have Learned

Activity 7g Writing the Language

Translate the following English sentences into Latin. Include all long marks. Use the stories and vocabulary lists in your textbook, as well as the vocabulary lists in this book, to help you:

1. Cornelius is writing letters in the country house.

   _____

2. The boys run into the woods, because they* want **(volunt)** to climb trees there.

   _____

3. Suddenly they* hear a voice.

   _____

4. A messenger comes toward them and says, "I am looking for Cornelius."

   _____

5. "The emperor is recalling the senators."

   _____

6. "It* is necessary to return to the city."

   _____

*Do not translate *they* or *it* with separate words.

Activity 7h Expanding Your English Vocabulary

Using the word bank on the next page, write the word that could replace the italicized word or words in each sentence. Use the Latin words in parentheses to help determine the meaning of the English words. Then write the English translation of each Latin word in the word bank:

1. The emperor has the power to *call back* a senator's privileges. _____

2. Wearing the toga was a well established *custom handed down* among Roman citizens. _____

3. The messenger's *greeting* to the boys was friendly. _____

4. The games in the arena attract many *observers*. _____

5. Cornelia enjoys her time in Baiae more than *city* life. _____

6. The visitor *declared* that he was a messenger from the emperor.   _____

7. The emperor's letter *brought forth* a groan of disappointment
from Cornelia.   _____

8. The messenger's *business* is to deliver the emperor's letters.   _____

9. The emperor composes *formal letters* to instruct the senators.   _____

10. The senator is a valued *advisor* to the emperor.   _____

tradition (**trādit**) _____	salutation (**salūtat**) _____
spectators (**spectant**) _____	urban (**urbem**) _____
revoke (**revocat**) _____	epistles (**epistulās**) _____
consultant (**cōnsulere**) _____	occupation (**occupātus**) _____
produced (**dūcit**) _____	announced (**nūntius**) _____

Activity 7i Reading Latin

Look at the new vocabulary beneath this story. Then read the story, noting subjects and direct objects as you meet them. Reread the story for comprehension. Then answer the questions that follow with complete Latin sentences:

What Is Happening?

In agrīs labōrant multī servī, quī in vīllā habitant. Servus, nōmine Geta, quī est miser et dēfessus, nōn labōrat sed sōlus sub arbore sedet. Īrātus est quod strēnuē labōrāre necesse est. Tum Dāvus ad servōs occupātōs venit. Omnēs strēnuē labōrant quod Dāvus vīlicus est. Geta tamen adhūc nōn labōrat quod Dāvum nōn timet. Dāvus Getam cōnspicit et clāmat, "Age, ignāve!" Nunc labōrat Geta īrātus.

Mox servī cōnspiciunt virum quī epistulās in sacculō habet. Vir puerōs et Cornēliam salūtat et ad eōs appropinquat. Servī vōcēs audīre nōn possunt quod vōcēs magnae nōn sunt. Geta, quī prope virum labōrat, arborem vīcīnam ascendit et vōcēs audit. Brevī tempore Mārcus et vir ad vīllam ambulant. Aliī servī revocant Getam, quī ex arbore dēscendit et ad eōs venit.

Dāvus, "Quis est vir?" inquit. "Est nūntius," respondet Geta. "Gāium Cornēlium petit."

Cūr nūntius Gāium Cornēlium petit? Quid accidit? Servī sollicitī sunt.

miser, *unhappy*
vīlicus, *overseer*
Age! *Come on!*
sacculō, *pouch, bag*
habet, *(he/she) has*
accidit, *is happening*

1. Quem Geta nōn timet?

_____

2. Quis epistulas in sacculō habet?

_____

3. Quōs vir salūtat?

_____

4. Quid Geta audit?

_____

5. Quem nūntius petit?

_____

GETTING UP EARLY

In addition to vocabulary and the story, the activities in this chapter focus on:

1. identifying the person and number of Latin verbs and translating them into English.
2. the forms of the irregular verb **sum**.
3. translating verbs.
4. vocative forms of nouns.

Vocabulary

Activity 8a Vocabulary

Study the vocabulary list on page 216 alone or with a partner. Note the personal pronouns. Go to the corresponding list on the Companion website where you will find the forms of the verbs **parō** *and* **sum**, *a list of other verbs that you have met that have forms like those of* **parō, parās**, *etc., and information on the forms of the vocative.*

The Story

Activity 8b Vocabulary in Context

Fill in the blanks with Latin words to match the English cues:

1. Aurēlia _____ occupāta est. (already)

2. "_____ hodiē strēnuē labōrāmus." (We)

3. "Cūr _____, servī, nōn labōrātis?" (you)

4. Aurēlia cubiculum Sextī _____. (enters)

5. Aurēlia Sextum _____ vult. (to wake up)

6. "_____, _____!" clāmat. ("Come on, Sextus!")

7. Sextus tunicam et togam _____. (puts on)

8. _____ ē cubiculō currit. (Then)

9. Aurēlia _____ Mārcī intrat. (bedroom)

10. Aurēlia _____ clāmat. (a second time)

11. "Cūr _____," inquit Mārcus, "necesse est surgere?" (for me)

12. "_____ _____ Rōmam redīre," clāmat Aurēlia.
    (It is time)

Forms

Verbs: Persons

Activity 8c Personal Endings

Write the personal endings for verbs that you would expect after these subjects:

1. tū _____

2. vōs _____

3. nōs _____

4. puerī _____

5. puella _____

6. ego _____

Activity 8d Person and Number

Identify the person (1st, 2nd, 3rd) and number (Sing. or Pl.) of the following verbs. Then translate each into English three ways, following the example that is done for you:

	Person	Number	Translation
1. vexās	*2nd*	*Sing.*	*you annoy, you are annoying, you do annoy*
2. vexāmus	_____	_____	_____
			_____
3. vexant	_____	_____	_____
			_____
4. vexō	_____	_____	_____
			_____
5. vexat	_____	_____	_____
			_____
6. vexātis	_____	_____	_____
			_____

Activity 8e The Verb *sum*

Write the forms of the verb **sum** *that you would expect after these subjects. Then translate each phrase:*

1. nōs _____ _____   **4.** vōs _____ _____

2. puerī _____ _____   **5.** puella _____ _____

3. ego _____ _____   **6.** tū _____ _____

Activity 8f Translating Verbs

Translate the following sentences into English, taking care to use the correct subject if there is no noun in the nominative case:

1. Servōs spectāmus.

_____

2. Mē vexātis, puerī.

_____

3. Cūr clāmās, Aurēlia?

_____

4. Cūr vīllam intrātis, Mārce et Sexte?

_____

5. Servī in cubiculīs nōn sunt.

_____

6. Servī aquam portant.

_____

7. Cūr nōn labōrātis, servī?

_____

8. "Tē ad urbem revocō," inquit nūntius.

_____

9. "Īrātus sum," inquit Cornēlius, "quod vōs, Mārce et Sexte, molestī estis."

_____

10. "Nōs dēfessī sumus," respondent puerī.

_____

Nouns and Adjectives: Vocative

Activity 8g Producing the Vocative Case

Give the Latin for the underlined words:

1. "Marcus, Cornelia, come here!"   _____

2. "Come here, boys!"   _____

3. Girls, why are you running to the tree?   _____

4. "Come here, <u>my son</u>!" _____

5. Why haven't you gotten up, <u>troublesome boy</u>? _____

6. <u>Slave</u>, why are you sitting? _____

7. I want to go to Rome now, <u>mother</u>. _____

8. <u>Cornelius</u>, everything is ready. _____

9. <u>Mothers and fathers</u>, please listen to us. _____

Underline the vocative forms in the sentences in Activity 8f.

Applying What You Have Learned

Activity 8h Writing the Language

Translate the following English sentences into Latin. Include all long marks. Use the stories and vocabulary lists in your textbook, as well as the vocabulary lists in this book, to help you:

1. The slaves are working hard because it is necessary to return to Rome today.

_____

_____

2. Marcus does not wish to get up because it is not yet light.

_____

_____

3. Cornelius enters the bedroom and shouts,

_____

_____

4. "Why don't you get up, Marcus? Why do you always annoy me?"

_____

_____

5. It is not necessary to shout a second time.

_____

_____

6. Marcus immediately gets up and puts on his* tunic and toga.

_____

_____

*Do not translate *his* with a separate word.

Activity 8i Expanding Your English Vocabulary

For each italicized English word below, give the related Latin word and below it the meaning of that Latin word. Then complete each sentence by filling in a word at the right:

Latin Word
Meaning of the Latin Word

If you ...

1. _____

tell an *exciting* story, it _____ the audience's interest.

_____

_____

2. _____

sleep in a *cubicle*, you sleep in a very small

_____

_____

3. _____

are *accelerating* in a vehicle, you are

_____

_____

4. _____

reiterate your words, you _____ them.

_____

_____

5. _____

are concerned with only *temporal* things, your interest is in things that exist for only a certain

_____

_____

Activity 8j Reading Latin

*Look at the new vocabulary following this story. Then read the story, noting the new personal endings on some of the verbs. Reread the story for comprehension. Then mark whether each statement below the story is V = **Vērum** or F = **Falsum**:*

Sextus Writes a Letter

Tuus fīlius Sextus s. d. (salūtem dīcit)

Laetus sum, mī pater! Ego et Mārcus et Cornēlia ad urbem īmus quod prīnceps, "Necesse est," scrībit, "Ō Cornēlī, ad urbem redīre." Hodiē ancillae tunicās et togās parant et meum cubiculum pūrgant.

Hodiē tamen Dāvum adiuvāre volō quod Dāvus mē amat. Saepe Dāvus, "Quō curritis, puerī?" clāmat. "Ubi estis, puerī? Ubi es, Sexte? Ubi est statua, Mārce? Agite! Tempus est in agrīs lūdere." Deinde respondēmus, "Sumus in hortō, Dāve. Statua in piscīnā est!"

Nōs et puellae in silvā saepe errāmus. Puellae, quod sunt perterritae, arborēs ascendere nōlunt, sed nihil mē terret. Saepe clāmāmus ego et Mārcus, "Lupōs timētis, puellae ignāvae! Abī, Cornēlia! Abī, Flāvia! Nōs puerī hīc lūdimus!"

Quid in Asiā facis, mī pater? Tūne tuum Sextum dēsīderās? Quamquam urbem vidēre volō, tē dēsīderō. Valē.

tuus, *your*	**nōlunt,** *(they) don't want*
fīlius, *son*	**hīc,** adv., *here*
salūtem dīcit, *says (sends) greetings*	**dēsīderās,** *you long for, miss*
īmus, *we are going*	**quamquam,** conj., *although*
lūdere, *to play*	**Valē!** *Goodbye!*

1. Sextus laetus est.   V   F

2. Puerī et Cornēlia ad urbem redīre parant.   V   F

3. Dāvus Sextum adiuvāre vult.   V   F

4. Puerī et Cornēlia et Flāvia in silvā saepe errant.   V   F

5. Puerī saepe clāmant, "Lupus puellās timet!"   V   F

6. Patrem vidēre Sextus nōn vult.   V   F

vult, *(he) wants*

GOODBYE

> *In addition to vocabulary and the story, the activities in this chapter focus on:*
> 1. ablative singular and plural forms of nouns.
> 2. prepositional phrases using nouns in the accusative and ablative cases.

Vocabulary

Activity 9a Vocabulary

Study the vocabulary list on pages 217–219 alone or with a partner. Note that we now give the ablative singular and plural of nouns and adjectives. Go to the corresponding list on the Companion website where you will find nominatives and ablatives of all 3rd declension nouns that you have met so far.

The Story

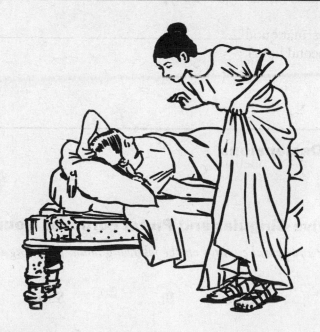

Activity 9b Vocabulary in Context

Fill in the blanks with Latin words to match the English cues:

1. Ubi Cornēlia ad vīllam amīcae currit, _____ eam videt. (no one)

2. Nōndum lūcet. _____ servī in agrīs labōrant. (No)

3. Cornēlia in vīllam amīcae _____ intrat. (silently)

4. Cornēlia est _____. (unhappy)

5. Cornēlia Flāviam _____ _____. (to wake up) (tries)

6. Flāvia, "_____ mē _____!" inquit. ("Don't wake...up!")

7. Cornēlia respondet, "_____! Venī _____ in agrōs!"
(Be quiet!) (with me)

8. "_____ necesse est ad urbem hodiē redīre." (for me)

9. Flāvia _____ _____ quod Cornēlia

_____. (unhappy) (weeps) (is going away)

10. Sed epistulās _____. (she promises)

11. Cornēlia, "_____!" inquit. ("Goodbye!")

12. Cornēlia Flāviam complexū _____ et brevī tempore

_____. (holds) (goes away)

13. Cornēlia ad vīllam festīnat quod _____ _____ discēdere
necesse est. (at the second hour)

Forms

Nouns: Cases and Declensions

Ablative Case

Activity 9c Ablative Singular and Plural Forms of Nouns

Fill in the ablative singular and plural endings on the following nouns according to their declension:

Sing.	**Pl.**	**Sing.**	**Pl.**	**Sing.**	**Pl.**
1. vōc_____,	vōc_____	**3.** puer_____,	puer_____	**5.** patr_____,	patr_____
2. serv_____,	serv_____	**4.** agr_____,	agr_____	**6.** puell_____,	puell_____

Building the Meaning

Prepositional Phrases: Accusative and Ablative Cases

Activity 9d Prepositional Phrases with Singular and Plural Nouns

A. *Add accusative or ablative singular endings as appropriate to complete the prepositional phrases in the following sentences. Be sure to identify the declension of each noun before deciding on its ending. Then translate the prepositional phrases in the blanks at the right:*

1. Flāvia in vīll_____ rūstic_____ habitat.   _____

2. Flāvia ex agr_____ currit.   _____

3. Flāvia aquam ad nūnti_____ portat.   _____

4. Urbs est prope rīv_____.   _____

5. Flāvia sub arbor_____ sedet.   _____

6. Nūntius epistulās per Itali_____ portat.   _____

7. Flāvia ē vīll_____ ambulat.   _____

8. Cornēlia in urb_____ intrat.   _____

9. Nūntius ex urb_____ advenit.   _____

B. *Add accusative or ablative plural endings as appropriate to complete the prepositional phrases in the following sentences. Be sure to identify the declension of each noun before deciding on its ending. Then translate the prepositional phrases in the blanks at the right:*

1. Puerī in arbor_____ ascendunt.   _____

2. Puerī in arbor_____ sedent.   _____

3. Amīcae ex agr_____ ambulant.   _____

4. Urbs est prope silv_____.   _____

5. Multī amīcī sub arbor_____ sedent.   _____

6. Puella per agr_____ errat.   _____

7. Puellae in vīll_____ vīcīn_____ habitant.   _____

8. Nūntius epistulās ad mult_____ urb_____ portat.   _____

9. Nūntiī ex urb_____ festīnant.   _____

Activity 9e Prepositional Phrases with *in* and with *ē/ex*:

Put parentheses around prepositional phrases. Then change the sentences to state the opposite by changing ē/ex to in and in to ē/ex. Be sure to identify the declension of each noun before deciding on its ending. The first one is done for you:

1. Puellae (in hortum) ambulant.

   Puellae ex hortō ambulant. _____

2. Puerī in agrōs currunt.

   _____

3. Nūntius ē vīllā festīnat.

   _____

4. Nōbīs in urbem īre necesse est.

   _____

5. Servī ex urbibus ambulant.

   _____

Activity 9f Longer Prepositional Phrases

Put parentheses around the prepositional phrases. Prepositional phrases can contain adjectives and conjunctions:

1. Flāvia sōla in magnā silvā vīcīnā errat.

2. Flāvia sub magnā arbore sedet et lacrimat.

3. Arbor est prope rīvum frīgidum.

4. Altera puella ad arborem et rīvum appropinquat.

5. "Salvē," inquit, "nunc in vīllā vīcīnā habitō."

6. Flāvia sub magnā arbore nōn iam lacrimat.

7. Tum puellae laetae per silvam et agrōs ambulant.

Underline all words in the ablative in the sentences above.

Applying What You Have Learned

Activity 9g Writing the Language

Translate the following English sentences into Latin. Include all long marks. Use the stories and vocabulary lists in your textbook, as well as the vocabulary lists in this book, to help you:

1. Flavia lives in a neighboring country house.

_____

2. Cornelia walks into the neighboring country house.

_____

3. Flavia and Cornelia no longer run in the fields.

_____

4. Now Flavia walks alone into the forest.

_____

5. Unhappy Flavia stays in the country house.

_____

Activity 9h Expanding Your English Vocabulary

Using the word bank on the next page, write the word that could replace the italicized word or words in each sentence. Use the Latin words in parentheses to help determine the meaning of the English words. Then write the English translation of each Latin word in the word bank:

1. The emperor's message *canceled* the vacation plans of Cornelius's family. _____

2. The *floor sweeper* here sometimes serves as a doorkeeper. _____

3. When Cornelia asked to be excused, Aurelia nodded her *silent* approval. _____

4. Aurelia *tried* repeatedly to wake up Marcus. _____

5. When Cornelius finished, Cornelia's face revealed her *unhappiness.* _____

6. When Aurelia called, the boys did not get up *at the same time.* _____

7. Flavia and Cornelia share a *tearful* farewell.   _____

8. Cornelia assures Flavia of her *enduring* friendship.   _____

9. Despite Sextus's *firmly held* grip, the branch broke and Sextus fell.   _____

10. The one boy talked a lot, but the other was *habitually silent*.   _____

misery (**misera**) _____	tacit (**tacitē**) _____
nullified (**nūllī**) _____	tenacious (**tenet**) _____
lachrymose (**lacrimat**) _____	simultaneously (**simul**) _____
janitor (**iānitor**) _____	attempted (**temptat**) _____
taciturn (**tacitē**) _____	permanent (**manēre**) _____

Activity 9i Reading Latin

Look at the new vocabulary following this story. Then read the story, noting prepositional phrases with the accusative and those with the ablative. Reread the story for comprehension. Then rewrite the prepositional phrases in the sentences below the story to make the statements true:

Flavia Is Left Behind

Ubi Cornēlia discēdit, Flāvia lacrimāns sub arbore stat. Puella misera lacrimat et ex agrīs ad vīllam tacitē ambulat. Ad iānuam vīllae iānitor sēmisomnus sedet. "Dormīsne?" rogat Flāvia. "Nōn dormiō!" iānitor īrātus magnā vōce respondet et statim surgit.

Flāvia vīllam intrat et mātrem petit. Per vīllam festīnat puella misera sed mātrem nōn videt. Flāvia ancillās in culīnā labōrantēs cōnspicit et rogat, "Quid facitis? Ubi est māter mea?" "Nescīmus," respondet ancilla occupāta. "Culīnam pūrgāmus neque mātrem tuam petere possumus."

Tandem vōcem audit Flāvia et in hortum festīnat. Mātrem prope piscīnam cōnspicit. Māter celeriter surgit. "Cūr lacrimās, mea fīlia?" rogat māter sollicita. "Ō mē miseram! Hodiē Cornēlia mea ad urbem redit et ego in vīllā maneō!" Māter fīliam complexū tenet. Brevī tempore Flāvia, "Necesse est mihi," inquit, "epistulam scrībere!" et ad cubiculum currit.

possumus, *we are able*   **fīlia,** *daughter*

1. Flāvia lacrimāns in agrōs tacitē ambulat.

   _____

2. "Nōn dormiō!" clāmat iānitor quī sub iānuā vīllae sedet.

   _____

3. Flāvia in hortō lentē ambulat et mātrem in piscīnā cōnspicit.

   _____

4. Dum Cornēlia ex urbe redit, Flāvia prope vīllam manet.

   _____

DEPARTURE

In addition to vocabulary and the story, the activities in this chapter focus on:
1. accusatives and infinitives used with **iubet** and **docet**.
2. infinitives and present tense forms of verbs of all conjugations.
3. regular and irregular imperatives.

Vocabulary

Activity 10a Vocabulary

Study the vocabulary list on pages 220–222 alone or with a partner. Go to the corresponding list on the Companion website where you will find a list of all the verbs that you have met so far.

The Story

Activity 10b Comprehension

Read through the Latin sentences below and number them in the order in which the actions they describe occur in the story in your textbook:

1. _____ Dāvus servōs iubet cistās in viam portāre.

2. _____ Cornēliī discēdunt.

3. _____ Sextus Getam reprehendit.

4. _____ Cornēlia in viam currit.

5. _____ Ancilla tunicās et stolās et pallās in cistam pōnit.

6. _____ Mārcus et Sextus in raedam ascendunt.

7. _____ Mārcus servōs incitat.

Building the Meaning

Accusative and Infinitive

Activity 10c Translating Sentences with *iubet* and *docet*

*Circle each infinitive used with **iubet** and **docet***. *Then translate the sentences:*

1. Prīnceps Cornēlium iubet Rōmam redīre.

   _____

2. Aurēlia Cornēliam docet tunicās parāre.

   _____

3. Aurēlia servōs iubet cistās portāre.

   _____

4. Sextus Getam reprehendit et servum docet cistās cūrāre.

   _____

5. Cornēlius omnēs iubet in raedam ascendere.

   _____

Forms

Verbs: Conjugations

Activity 10d Conjugations, Infinitives, and Translation of Verb Forms

Identify the conjugation to which each of the following verbs belongs, write its infinitive, and translate the verb at the left. The first is done for you:

	Conj.	Infinitive	Translation of the Verb at the Left
1. gemis	*3*	*gemere*	*you (sing.) groan, are groaning, do groan*
2. sedēmus			

3. stātis   _____   _____   _____

_____

4. audītis   _____   _____   _____

_____

5. facitis   _____   _____   _____

_____

6. timēs   _____   _____   _____

_____

7. dormīmus   _____   _____   _____

_____

8. currunt   _____   _____   _____

_____

Verbs: The Present Tense

Activity 10e Singular and Plural

Translate each of the following verb forms. Give the conjugation number of the verb. Then change the Latin forms from singular to plural or plural to singular, keeping the same person:

1. pōnō   _____   _____   _____

2. incitant   _____   _____

3. iacimus   _____   _____   _____

4. pōnis   _____   _____

5. iubeō   _____   _____

6. gerunt   _____   _____

7. cūrāmus   _____   _____

8. iacit   _____   _____

9. stās _____ _____ _____

10. pōnimus _____ _____ _____

11. vidēmus _____ _____ _____

12. cōnspicitis _____ _____ _____

13. dormīs _____ _____ _____

14. faciō _____ _____ _____

15. geritis _____ _____ _____

16. terrēs _____ _____ _____

17. iubent _____ _____ _____

18. audit _____ _____ _____

19. dormīmus _____ _____ _____

20. arripis _____ _____ _____

Verbs: Imperatives

Activity 10f Imperatives

Give the infinitives and the positive imperatives of the following verbs. Then give the corresponding negative imperatives for the first three sets:

	Infinitive	Singular Imperative	Plural Imperative
		Positive	Positive
		Negative	Negative
1. festīnō	_____	_____	_____
		_____	_____
2. dīcō	_____	_____	_____
		_____	_____
3. dūcō	_____	_____	_____
		_____	_____

4. veniō _____ _____ _____

5. promittō _____ _____ _____

6. faciō _____ _____ _____

7. iubeō _____ _____ _____

8. ferō _____ _____ _____

Activity 10g Issuing Orders

Write the Latin commands that would result in the following actions. Use vocatives and imperatives. The first set is done for you:

1. Mārcus raedam ascendit. *Mārce, raedam ascende!* _____

2. Puerī in raedam ascendunt. _____

3. Servī cistās in raedam iaciunt. _____

4. Ancillae ad raedam veniunt. _____

5. Puer baculum in raedam pōnit. _____

6. Puella mātrem audit. _____

7. Puer lupōs timet. _____

8. Sextus cistās portat. _____

9. Puellae rīdent. _____

10. Servus cistam in raedam nōn iacit. _____

11. Servī scelestī nōn dormiunt. _____

Applying What You Have Learned

Activity 10h Writing the Language

Translate the following English sentences into Latin. Include all long marks. Use the stories and vocabulary lists in your textbook, as well as the vocabulary lists in this book, to help you:

1. You are all working hard in the country house today.

_____

2. You (sing.) are getting the togas ready because senators usually wear a toga in the city.

_____

3. We usually wear a toga with purple border in the city.

_____

4. I am throwing the chest into the carriage.

_____

5. When all the chests are in the carriage, we climb in.

_____

Activity 10i Expanding Your English Vocabulary

For each italicized English word below, give the related Latin word and below it the meaning of that Latin word. Then complete each sentence by filling in a word at the right:

Latin Word
Meaning of the Latin Word

If you …

1. _____   *procrastinate* doing a chore, you put it
off until

_____

                                _____

2. _____   write an *itinerary*, you list the places
you will visit on a

_____

                                _____

3. _____   draw water from a *cistern*, you draw
water from a storage

_____

                                _____

4. _____   are the *proponent* of an idea, you are the one
who _____ it forward for discussion.

_____

                                _____

5. _____   *postpone* an appointment you _____ it   _____
off until a later date.

_____

6. _____ are an *alien*, you are a person from
   _____ country.   _____

   _____

7. _____ *incite* people to action, you _____
                          them to act.

   _____

8. _____ are involved in an *equestrian* sport, you
                          ride a   _____

   _____

9. _____ are an *itinerant* teacher, you _____
                          from one school to another.

   _____

10. _____ perform on gymnastic *apparatus*,
                           you perform on equipment _____   _____
                           for exercises.

   _____

Activity 10j Reading Latin

*Look at the new vocabulary following this story. Then read the story, noting the infinitives used with **iubet**, the personal endings of verbs, and the imperatives. Reread the story for comprehension. Then mark whether each statement is V = **Vērum** or F = **Falsum**:*

Davus

Dāvus ad iānuam vīllae stat et servōs Cornēliānōs spectat. Baculum habet et omnia cūrat. Servōs iubet cistās ad raedam ferre. Clāmat, "Cistās ad raedam ferte, servī!" "Cistās ad raedam ferimus," respondent servī.

Servum, nōmine Getam, iubet ad agrōs īre et aquam ad culīnam portāre. Dāvus clāmat, "Aquam, Geta, ex agrīs ad culīnam portā!" Geta gemit. "Aquam ex agrīs portāre nōlō," mussat servus, sed aquam ex agrīs petit.

Raedārium, nōmine Syrum, Dāvus vetat equōs vexāre. "Nōlī equōs vexāre, Syre!" clāmat. "Equōs nōn vexō," respondet Syrus.

Dāvus ancillās pallās et stolās in cistam pōnere iubet. "Pallās et stolās in cistam pōnite!" exclāmat sollicitus vīlicus. "Pallās et stolās in cistam pōnimus," respondent ancillae.

Aliī servī in hortō sedent. "Cūr sedētis neque labōrātis?" Dāvus īrātus clāmat. "Nōlīte sedēre, scelestī servī! Labōrāte strēnuē!" "Strēnuē labōrāmus," respondent servī.

"Nunc omnēs strēnuē labōrātis," inquit Dāvus.

"Tū quoque strēnuē labōrā!" mussant servī et ancillae.

vetō, vetāre, *to forbid*
mussō, mussāre, *to mutter*

1. Dāvus, "Cistās ferte!" inquit. Deinde servī cistās ferunt.   V   F

2. Dāvus, "Aquam portā!" inquit. Deinde Geta aquam portat.   V   F

3. Dāvus, "Equōs vexā!" inquit. Deinde raedārius equōs vexat.   V   F

4. Dāvus, "Pallās in cistam pōnite!" inquit. Deinde ancillae
   pallās in cistam pōnunt.   V   F

5. Dāvus, "Nōlīte labōrāre!" inquit. Deinde servī nōn labōrant.   V   F

A Slave Runs Away

In addition to vocabulary and the story, the activities in this chapter focus on:

1. genitive singular and plural forms of nouns.
2. using the genitive singular to identify the declension and base of a Latin noun and producing other case forms using this base.
3. determining whether nouns ending in *-ae* or *-ī* are genitive singular or nominative plural in sentences.

Vocabulary

Activity 11a Vocabulary

Study the vocabulary list on pages 223–224 alone or with a partner. Note that 1st and 2nd declension nouns are now given in the nominative singular with their genitive singular endings and genders. Third declension nouns are given with their genitive singular forms spelled out in full. For adjectives, nominative, genitive, accusative, and ablative forms are given in singular and plural for masculine and feminine. Go to the corresponding list on the Companion website where you will find a list of all the nouns that you have met so far, listed by declension with their genitive endings or genitive forms.

The Story

Activity 11b Vocabulary in Context

Fill in the blanks with Latin words to match the English cues:

1. Geta _____ nōn timet. (the master)

2. Ubi dominus _____, servī saepe nōn labōrant. (is away)

3. Geta _____ vult. (to run away, escape)

4. Nēmō eum _____. (hinders)

5. Geta _____ parat. (food)

6. _____ _____ ē vīllā fūrtim ambulat. (That night)

7. _____ nox est, servus celeriter currit. (Although)

8. Geta in silvam _____ arborum currit. (full)

9. In arbore _____ _____. (hides himself)

10. Dāvus servōs in _____ venīre iubet. (threshing floor)

11. Necesse est servōs _____, sī nōn strēnuē labōrant. (to beat)

12. Geta _____ vīlicī nōn timet. (the anger)

13. Dāvus ad _____ stat sed Getam neque vidēre neque audīre potest. (the gate)

14. _____ īrātus et sollicitus est. (the overseer)

Forms

Nouns: Cases and Declensions

Genitive Case

Activity 11c Genitive Singular and Plural Forms of Nouns

Fill in the genitive singular and plural endings on the following nouns according to their declension:

1. vōc_____, vōc_____   2. serv_____, serv_____   3. puer_____, puer_____

4. agr_____, agr_____   5. patr_____, patr_____   6. puell_____, puell_____

Activity 11d Identifying and Using Bases of Nouns

For each of the following nouns, draw a box around its base, circle the declension to which it belongs, and use its base to provide the requested form. The first one is done for you:

1. ager, agrī   1 ②3   nom. pl.   *agrī*

2. nūntius, nūntiī   1 2 3   gen. pl.   _____

3. arbor, arboris   1 2 3   acc. sing.   _____

4. iānua, iānuae   1 2 3   abl. pl.   _____

5. urbs, urbis   1 2 3   abl. sing.   _____

6. fīlia, fīliae   1 2 3   nom. pl.   _____

7. māter, mātris   1 2 3   abl. pl.   _____

8. ancilla, ancillae   1 2 3   abl. sing.   _____

9. vir, virī   1 2 3   acc. sing.   _____

10. vōx, vōcis   1 2 3   gen. pl.   _____

Building the Meaning

The Genitive Case

Activity 11e Putting Nouns into the Genitive Case

Make the following pairs of sentences say the same thing by filling in the blanks with appropriate words in the genitive case. Draw an arrow from each word in the genitive case to the noun it modifies. Translate each sentence. The first set is done for you:

1. Servus magnam īram habet.   *The slave has great anger.*

   Īra   *servī*   est magna.   *The anger of the slave/The slave's anger is great.*

2. Puella magnam vōcem habet. _____

   Vōx _____ est magna. _____

3. Pater longam epistulam habet. _____

   Epistula _____ est longa. _____

4. Puerī magnās cistās habent. _____

   Cistae _____ sunt magnae. _____

5. Puer equum strēnuum habet. _____

   Equus _____ est strēnuus. _____

6. Arborēs rāmōs īnfirmōs habent. _____

   Rāmī _____ sunt īnfirmī. _____

7. Puellae amīcās laetās habent. _____

   Amīcae _____ sunt laetae. _____

8. Servī vīlicum īrātum habent. _____

   Vīlicus _____ est īrātus. _____

9. Patrēs multōs servōs habent. _____

   Servī _____ sunt multī. _____

10. Sunt multī agrī. _____

    Numerus _____ magnus est. _____

Genitive Singular or Nominative Plural?
How Do You Decide?

Activity 11f Genitive Singular or Nominative Plural?

Read the following sentences. Decide whether the noun ending in -ae or -ī is genitive singular or nominative plural, and circle Gen. Sing. or Nom. Pl. If it is genitive singular, draw an arrow to the noun it modifies:

1. Cornēlius est dominus vīlicī et servōrum et ancillārum.

   vīlicī: Gen. Sing.   Nom. Pl.

2. Geta effugit et vīlicus Cornēliī est īrātus.

   Cornēliī: Gen. Sing.   Nom. Pl.

3. Diēs est calidus sed omnēs servī et ancillae in āreā stant.

   servī: Gen. Sing.   Nom. Pl.

   ancillae: Gen. Sing.   Nom. Pl.

4. Servī baculum vīlicī timent et tacitē stant.

   servī: Gen. Sing.   Nom. Pl.

   vīlicī: Gen. Sing.   Nom. Pl.

5. Īra vīlicī est magna; ancillae etiam sunt īrātae.

   vīlicī: Gen. Sing.   Nom. Pl.

   ancillae: Gen. Sing.   Nom. Pl.

6. Servī Cornēliī sunt īrātī.

   Servī: Gen. Sing.   Nom. Pl.

   Cornēliī: Gen. Sing.   Nom. Pl.

Applying What You Have Learned

Activity 11g Writing the Language

Translate the following English sentences into Latin. Include all long marks. Use the stories and vocabulary lists in your textbook, as well as the vocabulary lists in this book, to help you:

1. The carriage is full of boys and girls and is now departing.

   _____

   _____

2. Although Cornelius is absent, the slaves work hard in the master's country house and farm.

   _____

   _____

3. The anger of the overseer frightens the master's slaves.

   _____

4. The slaves fear the angry overseer's large stick, because he often beats them

   _____

   _____

5. Therefore they return to the fields.

   _____

Activity 11h Expanding Your English Vocabulary

Using the word bank on page 71, write the word that could replace the italicized word or words in each sentence. Use the Latin words in parentheses to help determine the meaning of the English words. Then write the English translation of each Latin word in the word bank:

1. The emperor's message roused the *anger* of the whole family. _____

2. Geta left ample evidence of his *nighttime* escape. _____

3. Marcus and Sextus *get in the way of* Davus's work in the garden. _____

4. The emperor holds the *controlling* power in Roman politics. _____

5. Davus will have to pursue the *fleeing* slave. _____

6. The emperor has called a *full* session of the Senate. _____

7. Cornelia could not *hide* her disappointment at the news. _____

8. The boys' shouts *resound* through the house. _____

9. Marcus defends Cornelia with *brotherly* devotion. _____

10. Cornelia will not forget the *numberless* joys of Baiae. _____

nocturnal (**nocte**) _____	dominant (**dominus**) _____
plenary (**plēnus**) _____	reverberate (**verberō**) _____
innumerable (**numerus**) _____	ire (**īra**) _____
impede (**impediō**) _____	fugitive (**effugiō**) _____
conceal (**cēlō**) _____	fraternal (**frāter**) _____

Activity 11i Reading Latin

Look at the new vocabulary beneath this story. Then read the story, mentally registering the forms of the words and their meanings as you read. Note all noun endings; four cases are used, including the genitive. Reread the Latin for comprehension of what is being said. Then answer the questions that follow the story with complete Latin sentences:

Davus Tells a New Slave about Cornelius's Family

Dāvus: Ego sum Dāvus, vīlicus Gāiī Cornēliī. Gāius Cornēlius est senātor Rōmānus et ad urbem saepe redit. Nunc dominus noster abest, sed hīc saepe habitat Cornēlius cum Aurēliā et Mārcō et Cornēliā et Sextō. Aurēlia est uxor Cornēliī.

Servus: Quis est Mārcus?

Dāvus: Mārcus est fīlius Cornēliī et frāter Cornēliae. Cornēlia igitur est soror Mārcī.

Servus: Sed quis est Sextus? Estne frāter Mārcī?

Dāvus: Minimē vērō! Nōn est frāter sed amīcus Mārcī. Pater Sextī est amīcus Cornēliī. Pater Sextī nōn iam in Italiā sed in Asiā habitat. Sextus cum Mārcō in Italiā habitat.

Servus: Suntne multī servī in familiā Cornēliānā?

Dāvus: Est magnus numerus servōrum et ancillārum. Aliī servī in vīllā labōrant, aliī in agrīs et vīneīs vīllae rūsticae.

Servus: Quid faciunt ancillae?

Dāvus: Vestēs līberōrum et parentum cūrant. Cibum quoque parant.

Servus: Ecce! Servī in vīllā rīdent. Suntne laetī servī Cornēliī? Amantne dominum?

Dāvus: Ita vērō! Ego sum vīlicus virī bonī.

> **familia, -ae,** f., *family, household*
> **vīnea, -ae,** f., *vineyard*
> **vestis, vestis,** f., *clothing*

1. Cuius fīlius est amīcus Sextī?

_____

2. Cuius amīcus est Mārcus?

_____

3. Cuius pater in Asiā habitat?

_____

4. Cūrantne ancillae vestēs Cornēliae et Mārcī et Sextī?

_____

5. Cuius servī sunt laetī?

_____

Cuius. . . ? *Whose . . . ?*

CAPTURE

> *In addition to vocabulary and the story, the activities in this chapter focus on:*
> 1. ablative singular and plural forms of nouns (review).
> 2. prepositional phrases with the ablative.
> 3. expressions of time, instrument or means, and manner with the ablative
>   without a preposition.

Vocabulary

Activity 12a Vocabulary

Study the vocabulary list on pages 225–226 alone or with a partner. Note the adjective **immōbilis,** *which has 3rd declension endings. Go to the corresponding list on the Companion website where you will find the ablative forms of sample 1st, 2nd, and 3rd declension nouns.*

The Story

Activity 12b Comprehension

Using the story in Chapter 12 of your textbook as a guide, read each sentence and circle **V** *for* **Vērum** *or* **F** *for* **Falsum.** *If the sentence is false, correct it by writing a sentence that is true below it:*

1. Ubi servī effugiunt, dominī vīlicōs nōn reprehendunt. V F

   _____

2. Dāvus servōs in āream statim convocat. V F

   _____

3. Dāvus servōs in vīllam mittit. V F

   _____

4. Dāvus servōs iubet canēs in āream dūcere. V F

   _____

5. Canēs veniunt et togam Getae olfaciunt et vēstīgia Getae inveniunt. V F

   _____

6. Rīvī et fossae canēs impediunt. V F

   _____

7. Clāmōrēs servōrum Getam excitant.   V   F

_____

8. Servī Getam in rāmīs arboris vident.   V   F

_____

9. Vīlicus Getam tunicā arripit et baculō verberat.   V   F

_____

10. Dominus servōs iubet in fronte Getae litterās FUG inūrere.   V   F

_____

Review

Activity 12c Ablative Case Endings

Write the declension number of each of these nouns. Then add the ablative singular and plural endings:

Declension	Ablative Singular	Ablative Plural
1. _____	can_____	can_____
2. _____	tunic_____	tunic_____
3. _____	vīlic_____	vīlic_____
4. _____	hort_____	hort_____
5. _____	arbor_____	arbor_____
6. _____	vīll_____	vīll_____
7. _____	agr_____	agr_____
8. _____	fīli_____	fīli_____
9. _____	sorōr_____	sorōr_____
10. _____	cist_____	cist_____

Building the Meaning

The Ablative Case

Activity 12d Prepositional Phrases and Expressions of Time, Instrument or Means, and Manner

Answer the following questions with full Latin sentences, using the words in parentheses as cues. The first question is answered for you:

1. Quandō servus effugit? (at night)

   Servus nocte effugit. _____

2. Unde servus effugit? (from the country house and farm)

   _____

3. Ubi servus sē cēlat? (in the branches of a tree)

   _____

4. Ubi petunt servī Getam? (in the garden, in the fields, in the vineyards)

   _____

5. Quibuscum Dāvus servōs in agrōs dūcit? (with dogs)

   _____

6. Quandō servī Getam inveniunt? (in a short time)

   _____

7. Quibuscum Dāvus ad arborem appropinquat? (with slaves and dogs)

   _____

8. Quō īnstrūmentō servī Getam inveniunt? (with dogs)

   _____

9. Quōmodo Dāvus clāmat? (with a loud voice)

   _____

10. Quō īnstrūmentō Dāvus Getam verberat? (with a stick)

   _____

Applying What You Have Learned

Activity 12e Writing the Language

Translate the following English sentences into Latin. Include all long marks. Use the stories and vocabulary lists in your textbook, as well as the vocabulary lists in this book, to help you:

1. At night the dogs are sleeping while Geta runs away.

_____

2. The slaves rouse the tired dogs and urge them on with sticks.

_____

3. The dogs hear Davus; the overseer shouts with great anger.

_____

4. The dogs smell Geta's tunic and run quickly with the slaves.

_____

5. Now the dogs lead many slaves out of the country house and farm through fields and streams.

_____

6. Look! The dogs bark because they catch the scent of Geta, who is in the tree.

_____

Activity 12f Expanding Your English Vocabulary

Using the word bank on page 77, write the word that could replace the italicized word or words in each sentence. Use the Latin words in parentheses to help determine the meaning of the English words. Then write the English translation of each Latin word in the word bank:

1. Eucleides' Greek accent revealed a *trace* of his Greek origin. _____

2. The carriage was *made motionless* by falling into a ditch. _____

3. Before buying new books, Eucleides makes a *list* of the books in his library. _____

4. The emperor demands a *calling together* of the senate. _____

5. Davus *questions* the slaves to discover the whereabouts of Geta. _____

6. Wolves belong to the *dog* family of animals. _____

7. Dogs have a keen *smelling* sense. _____

8. Davus *concludes* from the evidence that Geta has escaped. _____

9. Cornelius will *criticize* Davus because a slave escaped. _____

10. Davus *consults* with the rest of the slaves to find out when Geta
was last seen. _____

infers (**ferō**) _____	inventory (**inveniō**) _____
immobilized (**immōbilis**) _____	vestige (**vēstīgia**) _____
confers (**ferō**) _____	canine (**canis**) _____
convocation (**convocō**) _____	reprehend (**reprehendō**) _____
olfactory (**olfaciō**) _____	interrogates (**rogō**) _____

Activity 12g Reading Latin

Look at the new vocabulary beneath this story. Then read the story, noting uses of the ablative case with and without prepositions. Reread the story for comprehension. Then mark whether each statement following the story is V = Vērum or F = Falsum:

Thressa's Daughter Talks with Her Mother

Fīlia: Quandō nōbīs necesse est labōrāre, māter mea?

Thressa: Prīmā lūce nōbīs necesse est labōrāre. Saepe mediā nocte labōrāmus. Ēheu! Geta hodiē abest et Dāvus est sollicitus.

Fīlia: Ēheu! Geta est servus scelestus et ignāvus. Eum timeō.

Thressa: Quōmodo tē terret?

Fīlia: Īrātus saepe est et magnā vōce clāmat.

Thressa: Nunc Getam petit Dāvus.

Fīlia: Quibuscum eum petit Dāvus?

Thressa: Cum aliīs servīs et canibus Getam petit. Canēs vēstīgia Getae olfacere et Getam invenīre possunt.

Fīlia: Unde discēdunt servī et canēs?

Thressa: Ex āreā quae est prope vīllam discēdunt. Servī sunt sollicitī.

Fīlia: Quōmodo Getam petit Dāvus?

Thressa: Magnā cum dīligentiā Dāvus eum petit. Dāvus est vīlicus bonus et, ubi servus effugit, Dāvus eum invenit et verberat.

Fīlia: Quō īnstrūmentō eum verberat?

Thressa: Baculō eum verberat. Ecce! Quid audiō?

Servī et canēs redeunt et Dāvus Getam ad vīllam tunicā trahit. Mox vīlla plēna vōcum et clāmōris erit, nam servī litterās FUG in fronte Getae inūrent.

> **dīligentia, -ae,** f., *care*
>
> **erit,** *(it) will be*
>
> **inūrent,** *(they) will brand*

1. Ancillae prīmā lūce et mediā nocte saepe labōrant. V F

2. Geta magnā dīligentiā labōrat et omnēs magnā cum irā spectat. V F

3. Canēs Getam vēstīgiīs invenīre possunt. V F

4. Dāvus Getam magnā cum dīligentiā petit. V F

5. Dāvus Getam togā trahit et eum baculō verberat. V F

DISASTER

> *In addition to vocabulary and the story, the activities in this chapter focus on:*
> 1. the genitive plural of 3rd declension i-stem nouns.
> 2. 3rd person singular and plural forms of verbs in the imperfect tense.
> 3. adverbs.

Vocabulary

Activity 13a Vocabulary

Study the vocabulary list on pages 227–228 alone or with a partner. Note that we give the new imperfect forms of verbs. Go to the corresponding list on the Companion website where you will find a list of all the adverbs that you have met so far.

The Story

Activity 13b Vocabulary in Context

Fill in the blanks with Latin words to match the English cues:

1. Sextus in vehiculō cum _____ sedēbat. (the coachman)

2. Cornēlia _____ spectābat. (the peasants)

3. Aurēlia et Cornēlius in raedā _____. (were resting)

4. Rūsticī septimā _____ nōn iam labōrābant. (hour)

5. "Tabellārius, nōn _____, appropinquat," clāmat Mārcus. (a charioteer)

6. Tabellārius epistulās _____ _____ fert. (from the city)

7. Tabellāriī ad omnēs _____ Italiae festīnant. (parts)

8. Tabellārius epistulās _____ fert. (of citizens)

9. Tabellārius fatuus est, nam equōs _____ incitat. (fiercely)

10. "_____ tabellārium! Tenē equōs!" clāmat Sextus. (Watch out for . . .!)

Forms

3rd Declension i-stem Nouns

Activity 13c Genitive Plurals

Circle the nouns that are in the genitive plural:

aurīgārum   pedum   cīvium   puerum   servum   rūsticōrum   partium   tabellārium

Verbs: The Imperfect Tense I

Activity 13d Translating Verbs

Match each verb with the correct translation from the list on the right:

1. possunt _____   **a.** he was laughing

2. iacit _____   **b.** they are listening

3. rīdēbat _____   **c.** she is

4. currēbant _____   **d.** he is shouting

5. est _____   **e.** they kept running

6. audiēbant _____   **f.** they are able

7. currunt _____   **g.** she is laughing

8. clāmat _____   **h.** they were listening

9. erat _____   **i.** they are running

10. rīdet _____   **j.** he kept throwing

11. iaciēbat _____   **k.** she was shouting

12. poterant _____   **l.** he was

13. clāmābat _____   **m.** they were able

14. audiunt _____   **n.** she is throwing

Activity 13e Singulars, Plurals, and Translation
of Verbs in the Imperfect Tense

Change the imperfect verbs from singulars into plurals and plurals into singulars. Then translate the new verb:

1. volēbat _____ _____

2. erat _____ _____

3. ībant _____ _____

4. quiēscēbat _____ _____

5. verberābat _____ _____

6. dormiēbant _____ _____

7. ambulābant _____ _____

8. sedēbat _____ _____

9. iubēbant _____ _____

10. poterant _____ _____

Building the Meaning

Adverbs

Activity 13f Matching Adverbs with Meanings

Match the adverbs at the left with meanings at the right:

Adverbs		Meanings
1. celeriter	_____	**a.** not
2. crās	_____	**b.** no longer
3. deinde	_____	**c.** then, next
4. etiam	_____	**d.** silently
5. hīc	_____	**e.** also, even
6. hodiē	_____	**f.** however, nevertheless
7. mox	_____	**g.** now
8. nōn	_____	**h.** together, at the same time
9. nōn iam	_____	**i.** here
10. nunc	_____	**j.** also
11. quoque	_____	**k.** soon, presently
12. simul	_____	**l.** today
13. strēnuē	_____	**m.** quickly
14. subitō	_____	**n.** strenuously, hard
15. tacitē	_____	**o.** tomorrow
16. tamen	_____	**p.** suddenly

Activity 13g Adverbs in Sentences

Fill in the blanks with Latin adverbs to match the English cues:

1. Geta ē vīllā _____ currēbat. (stealthily)

2. Geta arborem ascendit et _____ sē cēlat. (there)

3. Dum per viam _____ ībant, māter et Cornēlia rūsticōs spectābant. (slowly)

4. In raedā māter et pater _____ dormiēbant. (already)

5. Mārcus _____ Cornēliam vexābat. (again)

6. Syrus equōs _____ verberābat. (again and again)

7. Quam _____ Syrus equōs verberat! (fiercely)

8. _____ Dāvus omnēs servōs excitat. (Meanwhile)

9. Dāvus est sollicitus, nam necesse est Getam _____ invenīre. (immediately)

10. Dominī vīlicōs nōn _____ verberant. (often)

11. Dominī servōs molestōs _____ verberant. (always)

12. Getam in fossīs _____ inveniunt. (not yet)

13. Geta _____ in arbore manet. (still)

14. _____ canēs Getam inveniunt. (Finally)

15. _____ Dāvus Getam verberat. (Then)

Applying What You Have Learned

Activity 13h Writing the Language

Translate the following English sentences into Latin. Include all long marks. Use the stories and vocabulary lists in your textbook, as well as the vocabulary lists in this book, to help you. Put all verbs into the imperfect tense:

1. Syrus was watching the peasants, who were resting silently under the trees.

_____

_____

2. He kept urging the horses on strenuously.

_____

3. "Come on!" the coachman was shouting again and again.

_____

4. A courier was quickly carrying letters of distinguished citizens.

_____

5. Syrus was able to avoid the courier, but not the ditch.

_____

_____

Activity 13i Expanding Your English Vocabulary

For each italicized English word below, give the related Latin word and below it the meaning of that Latin word. Then complete each sentence by filling in a word at the right:

Latin Word
Meaning of the Latin Word   **If you ...**

1. _____   know a result is *inevitable*, you know
   that it cannot be   _____

   _____

2. _____   are a *pedestrian*, you are   _____

   _____

3. _____   are enjoying a *quiescent* moment,
   you are taking a moment to   _____

   _____

4. _____   push a *pedal*, you press it with your   _____

   _____

5. _____   exercise your *civic* responsibilities,
   you perform the duties of a good   _____

   _____

6. _____   have *partitioned* something, you have
   divided it into   _____

   _____

7. _____   are *absent* from school, you have stayed
   away _____ it.   _____

   _____

8. _____   want to scare your opponent, you might
   roar *ferociously*. That is, you might roar   _____

   _____

9. _____   defend your *civil* rights, you defend
   your rights as a   _____

   _____

10. _____   follow a path of your own *volition*, you
    follow it because you _____ to.   _____

   _____

Activity 13j Reading Latin

Look at the new vocabulary beneath this story. Then read the story, noting the verbs in the imperfect tense. Reread the Latin for comprehension. Then correctly rewrite the sentences that follow the story:

Coming the Other Way

Celeriter iter faciēbat tabellārius quī epistulās cīvium praeclārōrum ferēbat. Equī erant dēfessī, sed tabellārius eōs identidem et ferōciter incitābat. "Necesse est," mussābat tabellārius sollicitus, "hodiē Neāpolim advenīre."

Mox raedam Cornēliānam procul cōnspicit.

"Ecce, raeda! Tarda et magna est. Ēheu! Ō mē miserum!" Deinde magnā vōce exclāmat, "Sed mihi necesse est festīnāre!" Equōs ferōciter incitat, et, ubi ad raedam appropinquat, identidem clāmat, "Tenē equōs tuōs, raedārie!"

Brevī tempore cisium tabellāriī raedam Cornēliānam magnā cum celeritāte praeterīre poterat. "Fatue!" mussābat tabellārius sed mox gemēbat quod equī nōn iam celeriter currēbant sed lentē et magnā cum difficultāte ambulābant. "Ēheu! Quid est? Equus claudus est. Necesse est mihi equum novum petere."

Neāpolim, *to/at Naples*	**praetereō, praeterīre,** *to go past*
procul, adv., *in the distance*	**difficultās, difficultātis,** f., *difficulty*
tardus, *slow*	**claudus,** *lame*
cisium, *light two-wheeled carriage*	**novus,** *new*
celeritās, celeritātis, f., *speed*	

1. Tabellārius epistulās mittēbat et iter lentē faciēbat.

   _____

2. Tabellārius hodiē Neāpolim advenīre nōlēbat.

   _____

3. Equī gemēbant quod nōn iam celeriter currēbant.

   _____

4. Necesse est cisium novum petere.

   _____

WHO IS TO BLAME?

In addition to vocabulary and the story, the activities in this chapter focus on:
1. imperfect tense forms of verbs of all conjugations and of **sum** and **possum**.
2. translating verbs in the imperfect tense at least four different ways in sentences.

Vocabulary

Activity 14a Vocabulary

Study the vocabulary list on pages 229–230 alone or with a partner.

The Story

Activity 14b Comprehension

Use the story in Chapter 14 of your textbook as a guide and circle **V** *for* **Vērum** *and*
F *for* **Falsum**: *If the sentence is false, correct it by writing a sentence that is true below it:*

1. Sextus ē raedā cadit.   V   F

_____

2. Cornēlius Sextum miserum reprehendit.   V   F

_____

3. Omnēs sunt incolumēs.   V   F

_____

4. Equī raedam ē fossā trahere possunt.   V   F

_____

5. Syrus in raedā dormiēbat.   V   F

_____

6. Cisium celerrimē appropinquābat.   V   F

_____

7. Syrus cisium vītāre nōn poterat.   V   F

_____

8. Mārcus omnia observābat.　　　　　　　　　　　　V　　F

_____

9. Erat culpa Syrī.　　　　　　　　　　　　　　　　V　　F

_____

10. Cornēlius Syrum virgā verberat.　　　　　　　　V　　F

_____

Forms

Verbs: The Imperfect Tense II

Activity 14c Imperfect Tense Forms

Fill in the imperfect endings to complete these sentences:

1. Vōs equōs spectā_____.

4. Puellae arborēs spectā_____.

2. Puella arborem spectā_____.

5. Nōs equum spectā_____.

3. Tū tabellārium spectā_____.

6. Ego viam spectā_____.

For each conjugation, fill in the vowel or vowels that come before the imperfect tense letters -ba-:

1st Conj.	2nd Conj.	3rd Conj.	3rd -iō Conj.	4th Conj.
_____	_____	_____	_____	_____

First decide to which conjugation each of the following verbs belongs, and then write the conjugation number after the verb. Then insert the correct vowel or vowels to complete each imperfect tense form:

1. arrip_____bat ___

5. tac_____bāmus ___

9. imped_____bant ___

2. err_____bam ___

6. ambul_____bātis ___

10. ten_____bās ___

3. dorm_____bās ___

7. mitt_____bam ___

11. clām_____bāmus ___

4. cad_____bant

8. gaud_____bam ___

12. extrah_____bam ___

Activity 14d Present to Imperfect

Change present tense forms to imperfect, keeping the same person and number:

1. movēs _____

2. concidunt _____

3. cessāmus _____

4. interpellātis _____

5. haeret _____

6. agō _____

7. arripis _____

8. appropinquat _____

9. trāditis _____

10. venīmus _____

Activity 14e Imperfect Verb Forms

Fill in the blanks with Latin verbs in the imperfect tense to match the English cues:

1. Cum raedāriō _____. (I was sitting)

2. In agrīs saepe _____. (we used to wander)

3. Puerī subitō _____. (began to laugh)

4. Tū togam praetextam _____. (used to wear)

5. Magnā arte raedam _____. (I kept driving)

6. Vōs cistās in raedam _____. (were throwing)

7. _____ ne in raedā, Syre? (Were you sleeping)

8. Cornēlius raedārium _____. (kept scolding)

9. Cisium celerrimē _____. (was approaching)

10. _____ quod omnēs erant incolumēs. (We were glad)

Activity 14f Translating the Imperfect

*The imperfect tense may be translated by English expressions indicating that the action (1)
was going on for a time, (2) was repeated, (3) was habitual, or (4) began to happen. Fill in the
blanks below with translations expressing these meanings:*

Rīdēbam =   1. I _____ laughing.   3. I _____ to laugh.

2. I _____ laughing.   4. I _____ to laugh.

Name _____ Date _____ Period _____

*Sometimes it makes better English to translate a verb in the imperfect tense in Latin with a verb in the simple past tense in English (e.g., **volēbam**, I wanted, and **nōlēbam**, I did not want). Translate the following sentences, using translations such as those above or a simple past when it makes better English. Sometimes more than one translation is possible:*

1. Mārcus canem habēbat.

_____

2. Cornēlia dormīre volēbat.

_____

3. Sextus diū vehicula spectābat.

_____

4. Dāvus identidem clāmābat.

_____

5. Raeda in fossā diū manēbat.

_____

6. Sextus in urbe Pompeiīs habitābat.

_____

7. Subitō Sextus currēbat.

_____

8. Mārcus omnia in Viā Appiā observābat.

_____

9. Cornēlia in raedā saepe dormiēbat.

_____

10. Cornēliī ad urbem iter faciēbant.

_____

Verbs: Irregular Verbs I

Activity 14g Present to Imperfect and Imperfect to Present

Change present tense forms to imperfect and imperfect tense forms to present, keeping the same person and number:

1. eram _____

2. potest _____

3. sumus _____

4. erātis _____

5. poterant _____

6. poterāmus _____

7. erās _____

8. possum _____

9. poterātis _____

10. erant _____

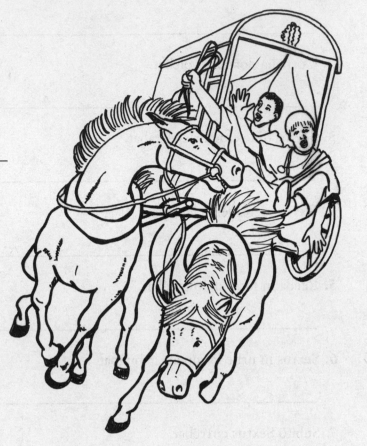

Applying What You Have Learned

Activity 14h Writing the Language

Translate the following English sentences into Latin. Include all long marks. Use the stories and vocabulary lists in your textbook, as well as the vocabulary lists in this book, to help you:

1. I was driving the carriage slowly.

_____

2. You, master, were sleeping in the carriage.

_____

3. Sextus was sitting here with me and watching the vehicles.

_____

4. A courier was traveling quickly.

_____

5. The danger was great, but we are all unhurt.

_____

Activity 14i Expanding Your English Vocabulary

Using the word bank below, write the word that could replace the italicized word or words in each sentence. Use the Latin words in parentheses to help determine the meaning of the English words. Then write the English translation of each Latin word in the word bank:

1. Sextus finds it difficult to *stick* to Cornelius's strict rules of conduct. _____

2. The horses are unable to *pull* the carriage *out* of the ditch. _____

3. The Cornelius family was the victim of a *chance event* on the road. _____

4. The peasants had *stopped* working and were resting under the trees. _____

5. Despite Sextus's explanation, Cornelius found Syrus *to blame.* _____

6. By reprimanding Syrus, Cornelius vented his *anger at the realization that his efforts were in vain.* _____

7. Syrus tried to keep the carriage out of *danger.* _____

8. Sextus tried to be a *"doer"* of justice in his defense of Syrus. _____

9. No one expected this to be such a *dangerous* journey. _____

10. The midday heat brought a temporary *stop* to their work. _____

extract (**extrahō**) _____	agent (**agō**) _____
peril (**perīculum**) _____	frustration (**frūstrā**) _____
adhere (**haereō**) _____	accident (**accidit**) _____
perilous (**perīculum**) _____	ceased (**cessō**) _____
cessation (**cessō**) _____	culpable (**culpa**) _____

Activity 14j Reading Latin

Look at the new vocabulary that follows this story. Then read the story, noting the personal endings of the verbs in the imperfect tense. Reread the story for comprehension. Then match the first parts of the sentences below the story to the clauses that correctly complete them:

From a Letter Written by Cornelia to Flavia

Dum in raedā per viam iter faciēbāmus, māter et pater dormiēbant. Ego quoque dormīre temptābam, sed Mārcus mē pede identidem vexābat et rīdēbat. Īrāta igitur mussābam, "Nōlī mē vexāre, moleste frāter! Pater saepe tē reprehendēbat quod identidem in lectō māne iacēbās neque surgēbās. Semper quoque reprehendēbat tē et Sextum quod in hortō currēbātis et Dāvum vexābātis. Nōlī patrem nunc tuīs iocīs excitāre!" Tandem nōn iam mē vexābat.

Nōs omnēs placidē dormiēbāmus ubi subitō audīmus Sextum, quī identidem clāmat, "Tenē equōs! Cavē fossam!" Statim omnia simul accidunt. Eucleidēs exclāmat. Raeda magnum frāgōrem facit. Māter et pater nōn iam dormiunt. Raeda in fossam dēscendit. Mārcus et māter ad sōlum raedae cadunt et gemunt. Ego lacrimābam. Quam perterritī erāmus!

Tandem omnēs tacitē sedēbāmus. Deinde lentē surgēbāmus et ē raedā dēscendēbāmus. Omnēs incolumēs erāmus, sed quam īrātus erat pater! Ō miserum raedārium!

> **māne**, adv., *in the morning*
> **iocus, -ī**, m., *joke, prank*
> **sōlum**, *floor*

1. Ubi māter et pater dormiēbant, _____

2. Cornēlius īrātus erat _____

3. Cornēliī subitō audiunt Sextum, _____

4. Ubi raeda in fossam dēscendit, _____

5. Quamquam omnēs incolumēs erant, _____

a. Cornēlia lacrimat.

b. Cornēlius īrātus erat.

c. per viam iter faciēbāmus.

d. quod Mārcus in lectō iacēbat.

e. quī identidem clāmat, "Tenē equōs!"

VEHICLE SPOTTING

In addition to vocabulary and the story, the activities in this chapter focus on:
1. the forms of neuter nouns.
2. noun look-alikes ending in *-a, -er, -um,* and *-us*.
3. the gender and case of each form of the words for *one, two,* and *three*.

Vocabulary

Activity 15a Vocabulary

Study the vocabulary list on pages 231–233 alone or with a partner. Note that we give all the neuter nouns that you have met so far and the neuter forms of adjectives. We also list the Roman numerals and numbers.

The Story

Activity 15b Vehicle Spotting

Circle each nominative or accusative neuter noun. Then translate the sentence into English:

1. Hodiē nōn sunt multa vehicula in Viā Appiā.

    _____

2. Puerī rotās audiunt et vehiculum cōnspiciunt.

    _____

3. Nōn est plaustrum quod onera magna nōn fert et celeriter appropinquat.

    _____

4. Plaustrum quattuor rotās habet, et bōvēs plaustra trahunt.

    _____

5. Nōn est raeda quod duās rotās, nōn quattuor, habet.

    _____

6. Vehiculum est cisium, et tabellārius in cisiō iter facit.

_____

_____

7. Cisium celeriter praeterit, et Cornēliī adhūc in fossā manent.

_____

8. Nunc puerī vēstīgia rotārum in viā vident.

_____

Forms

Neuter Nouns

Activity 15c Forms of Neuter Nouns

Fill in the forms of **cisium** *in the singular and of* **onus** *in the plural:*

cisium	**Singular**	*onus*	**Plural**
Nom.	_____	Nom.	_____
Gen.	_____	Gen.	_____
Acc.	_____	Acc.	_____
Abl.	_____	Abl.	_____

Activity 15d Identifying Noun Look-Alikes

Neuter nouns can be confused with nouns of other genders. Identify the declensions, genders, possible cases, and numbers of the nouns below by circling the appropriate responses. Some nouns could be more than one gender or case:

	Declension	**Gender**	**Possible Cases**	**Number**
1. bacula	1 2 3	m. f. n.	nom. gen. acc. abl. voc.	sing. pl.
2. rota	1 2 3	m. f. n.	nom. gen. acc. abl. voc.	sing. pl.
3. cisia	1 2 3	m. f. n.	nom. gen. acc. abl. voc.	sing. pl.

4. puer	1	2	3	m.	f.	n.	nom.	gen.	acc.	abl.	voc.	sing. pl.
5. iter	1	2	3	m.	f.	n.	nom.	gen.	acc.	abl.	voc.	sing. pl.
6. ager	1	2	3	m.	f.	n.	nom.	gen.	acc.	abl.	voc.	sing. pl.
7. perīculum	1	2	3	m.	f.	n.	nom.	gen.	acc.	abl.	voc.	sing. pl.
8. hortum	1	2	3	m.	f.	n.	nom.	gen.	acc.	abl.	voc.	sing. pl.
9. cīvium	1	2	3	m.	f.	n.	nom.	gen.	acc.	abl.	voc.	sing. pl.
10. plaustrōrum	1	2	3	m.	f.	n.	nom.	gen.	acc.	abl.	voc.	sing. pl.
11. aurīgārum	1	2	3	m.	f.	n.	nom.	gen.	acc.	abl.	voc.	sing. pl.
12. clāmōrum	1	2	3	m.	f.	n.	nom.	gen.	acc.	abl.	voc.	sing. pl.
13. tempus	1	2	3	m.	f.	n.	nom.	gen.	acc.	abl.	voc.	sing. pl.
14. onus	1	2	3	m.	f.	n.	nom.	gen.	acc.	abl.	voc.	sing. pl.
15. rāmus	1	2	3	m.	f.	n.	nom.	gen.	acc.	abl.	voc.	sing. pl.

Activity 15e Identifying Noun Look-Alikes in Sentences

Answer the questions under each sentence. Then translate the sentence into English:

1. Puella vehicula cōnspicit.

   Why can **vehicula** not be the subject of the sentence?

   _____

   _____

   Translation:_____

2. Onera vehicula portant.

   How can you decide which word is the subject of this sentence?

   _____

   _____

   Translation:_____

3. Puer ad urbem iter facit.

How can you decide whether **puer** or **iter** is the subject of this sentence?

_____

_____

Translation:_____

4. Vīllae Rōmānae cubicula habent.

Since both **vīllae** and **cubicula** could be plural, how can you tell which would be the subject of the plural verb?

_____

_____

Translation:_____

5. Vēstīgia lupī puellae vident.

How can you tell whether **vēstīgia, lupī**, or **puellae** is the subject of the plural verb?

_____

_____

Translation:_____

6. Silentium puerum terret.

How can you decide which noun is the subject of this sentence?

_____

_____

Translation:_____

7. Īra patrum puellās terret.

How can you decide what is the subject of this sentence?

_____

_____

Translation:_____

8. Cisium in viā audiō.

Why can **cisium** not be the subject of this sentence?

_____

_____

_____

Translation:_____

9. Auxilium Cornēliī nōn inveniunt.

IIow can you decide what is the subject of this sentence?

_____

_____

Translation:_____

10. Servus onus portat.

Why can **onus** not be the subject of the sentence?

_____

_____

Translation:_____

Forms

Roman Numerals and Latin Numbers

Activity 15f Gender and Case of the Latin Words for One, Two, and Three

Circle each of the words for numbers used in the sentences below and use abbreviations to write its gender and case on the lines provided:

1. Duo līberī ūnam mātrem habent. _____ _____ _____

2. Sextus cum duōbus līberīs habitat. _____ _____

3. Māter et pater et līberī cum tribus canibus habitant. _____ or _____ _____

4. Līberī duōs ex canibus amant. _____ _____

5. Flāvia est amīca trium līberōrum. _____ _____

6. Vīlla rūstica tria cubicula habet. _____ _____

7. Duō parentēs duās vīneās et duō olīvēta habent. _____ _____ _____ _____

Applying What You Have Learned

Activity 15g Writing the Language

Translate the following English sentences into Latin. Include all long marks. Use the stories and vocabulary lists in your textbook, as well as the vocabulary lists in this book, to help you:

1. The boys were able to see the tracks of two vehicles.

_____

_____

2. Two wagons were carrying large loads.

_____

3. Two children hear the rumble of five carriages.

_____

_____

4. Three children and two parents were making the journey to the city in one carriage.

_____

_____

5. A **cisium** has only two wheels.

_____

Activity 15h Expanding Your English Vocabulary

For each italicized English word below, give the related Latin word and below it the meaning of that Latin word. Then complete each sentence by filling in a word at the right:

Latin Word   **If you ...**
Meaning of the Latin Word

1. _____   *expect* a result, you _____ for it.   _____

_____

2. _____   show *apparent* enthusiasm, you show
                                 enthusiasm that _____ to be genuine.   _____

_____

3. _____   *rotate* an object, you _____ it around.   _____

_____

4. _____   do an *onerous* task, you do a task that is   _____

_____

5. _____   are looking at a *bovine* face, you see a face
                                 that has features similar to those of an   _____

_____

6. _____   are *tardy* for an appointment, you arrive   _____

_____

7. _____   are measuring *longitude*, you are using
                                 the _____ imaginary lines running   _____
_____   from the north pole to the south pole.

8. _____ *unify* separate peoples, you bring them
   _____ together into _____ group.   _____

9. _____ behave with *duplicity*, you might be
                          accused of being _____ faced.   _____

10. _____ ask the *quota* of fish allowed to be caught
                          per day, you are asking _____ you
    _____ are allowed to catch.   _____

Activity 15i Reading Latin

Look at the new vocabulary beneath this story. Then read the story. Note which nouns are neuter, and note their cases and their functions in their sentences. Reread the story for comprehension. Then correctly rewrite the sentences on the next page:

Worried and Waiting

Dum Sextus et Mārcus vehicula exspectant, duo parentēs sollicitī silentiō stant. Tandem Cornēlius īrātus, "Nostra raeda," inquit, "onus magnum portābat. Equī dēfessī eam frūstrā ē fossā extrahere temptant. Syrus raedam movēre nōn potest. Necesse est nōbīs auxilium invenīre."

"Ubi auxilium invenīre possumus?" rogat Aurēlia. "Nūllum vehiculum in viā appāret. Vidēsne rūsticōs aut bovēs in agrīs vīcīnīs?" Cornēlius, "Rūsticōs videō," inquit, "sed occupātī sunt quod bovēs plaustra plēna onerum trahunt."

"Ecce, pater!" subitō clāmat Cornēlia, quae ad eōs currit. "Quid in viā est?" Procul est nūbēs pulveris. Omnēs murmur rotārum audīre possunt. Cornēlius, "Fortasse est," inquit, "vehiculum." "Fortasse," inquit Aurēlia laeta, "est vir praeclārus cum multīs servīs!" Mox murmur est magnum. "Fortasse est raeda cum quattuor equīs," inquit Cornēlius. Dum vehiculum praeterit, Cornēlius clāmat, "Fer nōbīs auxilium! Fer auxilium!"

Nōn raeda tamen, sed cisium est et celeriter praeterit. Cornēlius gemit. Intereā Syrus duōs equōs dēfessōs virgā identidem verberat.

silentiō, *silently*
aut, conj., *or*

1. Syrus equōs dēfessōs ē fossā extrahere temptat.

_____

2. Aurēlia nūllum onus in viā cōnspicit.

_____

3. Bovēs raedam plēnam equōrum in agrīs trahunt.

_____

4. Cornēliī auxilium procul audiunt.

_____

5. Vehiculum magnō silentiō appropinquat.

_____

6. Cisium tardē praeterit.

_____

WHY IS SEXTUS A PEST

In addition to vocabulary and the story, the activities in this chapter focus on:
1. forms of 1st and 2nd declension adjectives.
2. agreement of adjectives with nouns of the 1st, 2nd, and 3rd declensions in gender, case, and number.

Vocabulary

Activity 16a Vocabulary

Study the vocabulary list on pages 234–235 alone or with a partner. Go to the corresponding list on the Companion website where you will find a list of all the 1st and 2nd declension adjectives that you have met so far.

The Story

Activity 16b Dictation and Vocabulary

Fill in the blanks as your teacher reads the story aloud. Then go back and write the meanings of the Latin words in the spaces provided. As you do so, add pronouns as subjects for any verbs that do not have expressed subjects in the Latin:

Iam **1.** _____ _____ = _____

_____ erat. Adhūc immōbilis in fossā haerēbat raeda. Sed nihil

facere Sextum **2.** _____ = _____, nam puer

strēnuus erat. Subitō igitur ad raedam currit et cistam **3.** _____ =

_____. Tum ē cistā **4.** _____ =

_____ extrahit. **5.** "_____ = _____

pilā **6.** _____ = _____, Mārce?" clāmat. Pilam ad

Mārcum statim iacit. Mārcus eam **7.** _____ = _____

et ad Sextum mittit. Identidem puerī pilam iaciēbant, **8.** _____ =

_____ ad **9.** _____ = _____.

Tum Sextus, quī semper Cornēliam vexāre vult, **10.** _____

_____ = _____ pilam iacit et Cornēliam

11. _____ = _____.

Statim īrāta Cornēlia ad mātrem sē 12. _____ =

_____ et, "Cūr mē semper vexat Sextus, māter?" clāmat. "Cūr pilam

in mē iacit? Quam molestus puer est Sextus!"

"Venī ad mē, 13. _____ = _____," respondet

māter et fīliam complexū tenet. "Sextus tē ferīre in 14. _____ =

_____ nōn habēbat. Est puer strēnuus, est puer temerārius, nōn tamen

est puer scelestus."

"Sed cūr Sextus 15. _____ = _____ nōs

habitat?" rogat Cornēlia, quae adhūc īrāta est. "Cūr pater Sextī eum ad nōs mittit?"

"Pater Sextī ad Asiam iter facit. Quod pater abest, necesse erat Sextum in Italiā

16. _____ = _____. 17. _____

= _____, quod pater Sextī 18. _____ =

_____ patris tuī est, Sextus apud nōs manet."

"Quid tamen 19. _____ _____ =

_____ Sextī?" rogat fīlia. "Cūr 20. _____ =

_____ fīlium nōn cūrat?"

"Ēheu!" respondet Aurēlia. "Māter Sextī, ut scīs, iam 21. _____ =

_____ est. Mātrem nōn habet Sextus." Tacēbat Cornēlia, nōn iam īrā

commōta.

Eō ipsō tempore tamen Sextus, "Vīsne 22. _____ =

_____ lūdere, Cornēlia?" exclāmat. "Quamquam tū es puella,

23. _____ = _____ iacere fortasse potes." Dum

clāmābat, iam rīdēbat et effugiēbat. Iterum īrāta Cornēlia, "Abī, moleste puer!" clāmat.

"24. _____ _____ = _____ nōlō."

Building the Meaning

Nouns and Adjectives: Agreement I

Activity 16c Agreement of Nouns and Adjectives

Circle the adjectives that agree with the underlined nouns. Remember that adjectives are always the same gender, case, and number as the nouns they modify but that the adjective and its noun will not necessarily have identical endings. Then translate the sentences:

1. Cornēlius īrātus in viā ambulābat et (alius / alia / aliud) <u>vehiculum</u> exspectābat.

_____

2. Iterum <u>pater</u> (sollicitum / sollicitō / sollicitus) raedam quae erat in fossā spectābat et gemēbat.

_____

3. (Nūllus / Nūlla / Nūllum) <u>vehiculum</u> appāret.

_____

4. Pater (magnōs / magnās / magnae) <u>clāmōrēs</u> Sextī prope raedam audiēbat.

_____

5. Statim <u>pater</u> īrā (commōtus / commōtā / commōtum) puerum molestum reprehendēbat.

_____

6. <u>Puer</u> (perterrita / perterritum / perterritus) nunc tacet et nōn iam pilā lūdit.

_____

7. Eucleidēs (magnōs / magnās / magnī) <u>vōcēs</u> neque Cornēliī neque puerōrum audit quod librum legit.

_____

8. Cornēlia cum mātre sub (magnā / magnō / magnus) <u>arbore</u> sedet.

_____

9. <u>Māter</u> (sollicitus / sollicita / sollicitum) fīliam complexū tenet.

_____

10. Subitō Cornēliī (magnus / magnum / magnam) <u>fragōrem</u> audiunt.

_____

11. <u>Rāmus</u> (īnfirmus / īnfirmās / īnfirmōs) ex arbore cadit.

_____

12. <u>Cornēliī</u> sunt incolumēs sed (perterritīs / perterritōs / perterritī).

_____

13. <u>Diēs</u> erat (calida / calidus / calidum), sed nunc <u>nox</u> (frīgida / frīgidus / frīgidum) appropinquat.

_____

14. <u>Senātor</u> nunc est (sollicita / sollicitō / sollicitus) quod <u>nox</u> (perīculōsus / perīculōsa / perīculōsum) venit.

_____

Applying What You Have Learned

Activity 16d Writing the Language

Translate the following English sentences into Latin. Include all long marks. Use the stories and vocabulary lists in your textbook, as well as the vocabulary lists in this book, to help you:

1. To sit in the road bored the children.

_____

2. Sextus finds a ball in a chest and plays ball with Marcus.

_____

3. But Sextus is often an annoying boy and (he) hits Cornelia with a ball.

_____

4. Cornelia is angry and turns toward her mother.

_____

5. "Sextus is not a wicked boy," replies Aurelia, "but he is anxious because his mother is dead. He wasn't intending to hit you."

_____

Activity 16e Expanding Your English Vocabulary

Using the word bank below, write the word that could replace the italicized word or words in each sentence. Use the Latin words in parentheses to help determine the meaning of the English words. Then write the English translation of each Latin word in the word bank:

1. Aurelia *turned away* her eyes from the accident. _____

2. The boys soon turned even this event into *merry good fun*. _____

3. Sextus found it *boring* merely to wait at the side of the road. _____

4. Cornelius had to make a *change* in his plans. _____

5. Syrus was *deceived* into thinking the courier would yield. _____

6. Cornelius gave *voiced* expression to his anger. _____

7. The Cornelius family took in Sextus as a gesture of *welcoming a friend*. _____

8. Cornelius was in no mood to *let go of* his anger. _____

9. Aurelia was upset by the experience of *deadly* danger. _____

10. Water was leaking from a small *opening* in the jar. _____

---

vocal (**vocō**) _____   deluded (**lūdō**) _____

tedious (**taedēbat**) _____   jocularity (**iocus**) _____

aperture (**aperiō**) _____   mortal (**mortuus**) _____

relinquish (**relinquō**) _____   hospitality (**hospes**) _____

averted (**vertō**) _____   alteration (**alter...alterum**) _____

Activity 16f Reading Latin

Look at the new vocabulary beneath this story. Then read the story, noting noun-adjective pairs, especially those with words of different declensions. Reread the story for comprehension. Then answer the questions on the next page with complete Latin sentences:

Taking a Break

Syrus et alius servus, nōmine Eucleidēs, prope raedam manent. Syrus equōs nōn iam incitat sed ad Eucleidem lentē ambulat. Duo servī in viā cōnsīdunt.

Eucleidēs: Cūr equōs nōn iam incitās, Syre? Dominus noster est vir bonus sed adhūc īrātus est.

Syrus: Diū equōs dēfessōs virgā verberābam, sed frūstrā. Ut vidēs, equī īnfirmī et paene mortuī sunt. Tempus est quiēscere. Quid faciēbās tū, mī amīce, dum ego equōs incitābam?

Eucleidēs: Raeda magnum onus ferēbat. Cistās familiae nostrae movēbam et in agrō vīcīnō pōnēbam.

Syrus: Erantne in raedā multae cistae?

Eucleidēs: In vehiculō erant multae cistae sed nōn magnae.

Syrus: Cuius cista aperta est?

Eucleidēs: Cista Sextī aperta est. Puer ē cistā pilam extrāxit. Puerī nunc pilā lūdunt. Ecce! Noster Mārcus pilam magnā arte iacit et excipit.

Syrus: Ita vērō! Bonus puer est Mārcus. Quid dē Cornēliō? Quid in animō facere habet Cornēlius? Habetne hospitem quī prope habitat?

Eucleidēs: Hospitem vīcīnum dominus noster nōn habet. Apud hospitem pernoctāre nōn possumus.

Syrus: Ēheu! Ego in viā cum raedā et equīs dēfessīs sōlus pernoctāre nōlō.

cōnsīdō, cōnsīdere, *to sit down*

paene, adv., *almost*

familia, -ae, f., *family, household*

Cuius...? *Whose...?*

apertus, -a, -um, *open*

extrāxit, *took out*

prope, adv., *nearby*

pernoctō, pernoctāre, *to spend the night*

1. Quālem dominum habent Syrus et Eucleidēs?

_____

2. Quālēs equōs verberābat Syrus?

_____

3. Quāle onus in raedā est?

_____

4. Quālem artem habet Mārcus ubi pilā lūdit?

_____

5. Cūr ad hospitem vīcīnum nōn iter facit Cornēlius?

_____

DO WE STAY AT AN INN?

In addition to vocabulary and the story, the activities in this chapter focus on:

1. present and imperfect forms of verbs of all four conjugations (review)

2. present and imperfect forms of irregular verbs:

   eō, īre, *to go*

   ferō, ferre, *to bring, carry, bear*

   nōlō, nōlle, *not to wish, not to want, to be unwilling*

   possum, posse, *to be able; I can* (review)

   sum, esse, *to be* (review)

   volō, velle, *to wish, want, be willing*

Vocabulary

Activity 17a Vocabulary

Study the vocabulary list on page 236 alone or with a partner. Note the list of irregular verbs.

The Story

Activity 17b Comprehension

The story in Chapter 17 contains a great deal of dialogue. Without looking in your textbook, match the quotations below with the characters who said them. Write A for Aurelia, C for Cornelius, and E for Eucleides. The quotations do not appear in the same order as they do in your textbook.

1. _____ Cūr timēs, mea domina?

2. _____ Necesse est igitur ad caupōnam īre.

3. _____ Senātōrēs Rōmānī in caupōnīs nōn pernoctant.

4. _____ Caupōnās nōn amō. Saepe ibi perīcula sunt magna.

5. _____ Ō mē miseram!

6. _____ Hīc in Viā Appiā pernoctāre nōn possumus.

7. _____ Vidēsne illud aedificium, domine?

8. _____ Fortasse equī caupōnis raedam ē fossā extrahere possunt.

9. _____ Ille caupō est amīcus meus.

10. _____ Agite, puerī!

Forms

Verbs: Regular Verbs (Review)

Activity 17c Present Tense (Review of Regular Verbs)

Complete the following sentences with present tense forms of the given verbs. Cues are given with the first set only. For the others, you will need to choose the correct person and number for the verb from the sense of the sentence as a whole and its context:

videō, vidēre

1. Eucleidēs aedificium _____. (sees)

2. "_____ illud aedificium, domine?" inquit Eucleidēs. (Do you see)

3. "Ita vērō! Id _____," inquit Cornēlius. (I see)

4. "_____ illud aedificium, Aurēlia et Cornēlia?" (Do you see)

5. "Nōs aedificium nōn _____," inquiunt Aurēlia et Cornēlia. (do . . . see)

6. Puerī quoque aedificium nōn _____. (do . . . see)

audiō, audīre

7. "_____ murmur rotārum, Sexte?" rogat Mārcus.

8. "Murmur rotārum nōn _____," respondet Sextus.

9. "_____ canem procul lātrantem, puerī?" rogat Cornēlius.

10. "Ita vērō, canem lātrantem _____," respondent puerī.

11. Aurēlia et Cornēlia canem lātrantem nōn _____.

12. "Canem lātrantem nōn _____," inquiunt Aurēlia et Cornēlia.

petō, petere

13. Rūsticus Cornēliōs videt et rogat, "Quid vōs _____?"

14. "Nōs caupōnam _____," respondet Cornēlius.

15. "_____ illam caupōnam!" clāmat rūsticus.

16. Cornēliī caupōnam _____.

ambulō, ambulāre

17. Cornēlia cum Eucleide _____.

18. "Quō nōs _____?" rogant Cornēlia et puerī.

19. "Vōs ad caupōnam _____," respondet Eucleidēs.

20. "Quō _____, rūstice?" rogat Cornēlius.

21. "Ad urbem Neāpolim _____," respondet rūsticus.

Activity 17d Imperfect Tense

Change the verbs in the following sentences from the present to the imperfect and translate the new sentences:

1. Raeda in fossā haeret (_____).

   _____

2. "Cornēlia, quid legis (_____)?"

   _____

3. Caupō multōs equōs habet (_____).

   _____

4. Equī Cornēliī raedam ē fossā nōn extrahunt (_____).

   _____

5. "Pernoctātisne (_____) in caupōnā?"

_____

6. Equōs ad caupōnam dūcis (_____).

_____

7. Raedārius in viā manet (_____).

_____

8. "Custōdīsne (_____) equōs in viā?"

_____

9. "Ita vērō, custōdiō (_____) equōs in viā."

_____

10. Cornēliī in caupōnā pernoctant (_____).

_____

11. Cornēliī ē vīllā rūsticā veniunt (_____).

_____

12. Rūsticī in agrīs labōrant (_____).

_____

13. In viā cum Mārcō pilā lūdō (_____).

_____

14. Ad caupōnam in Viā Appiā ambulāmus (_____).

_____

15. Magnā vōce "Auxilium ferte!" clāmāmus (_____) quod perīculum est
(_____) magnum.

_____

Verbs: Irregular Verbs II

Activity 17e Irregular Verbs (Present Tense)

Translate the following sentences into English:

1. "Cūr in caupōnā pernoctāre nōn vultis?"

   _____

2. "In caupōnā pernoctāre nōlumus quod caupōnae perīculōsae sunt."

   _____

3. "Quō īs et quid fers?"

   _____

4. "Ad caupōnam eō, et cistam meam ferō."

   _____

5. Tabellārius celeriter per viam it.

   _____

Activity 17f Irregular Verbs (Present Tense)

Complete the following sentences with the correct present tense form of the verb in parentheses.
Use the sense of the sentence to determine what person and number the verb should be:

1. Sextus, "Ego," inquit, "prope raedam sedēre _____." (not to want)

2. "Quō _____, Sexte?" rogat Mārcus. (to go)

3. Sextus pilam in viā _____. (to carry)

4. Sextus Mārcum rogat, "_____ ne tū pilā lūdere?" (to want)

5. Mārcus, "Ita vērō," inquit, "pilā lūdere _____!" (to want)

Activity 17g Irregular Verbs (Imperfect Tense)

Look carefully at the endings of the verbs to determine the subjects of these sentences. Then translate the sentences into English:

1. Rōmam ībāmus.

   _____

2. Raedārius virgam ferēbat.

   _____

3. Cibum in raedā ferēbātis.

   _____

4. In fossā manēre nōlēbāmus.

   _____

5. In vīllā hospitis pernoctāre volēbātis.

   _____

Activity 17h Irregular Verbs (Imperfect Tense)

Complete the following sentences with the correct Latin form of the verb in parentheses, using the imperfect tense. Use the sense of the sentence to determine what person and number the verb should be:

1. Cornēlius in viā nocte manēre _____. (not to wish/want)

2. "Nōs in caupōnā manēre _____." (not to wish/want)

3. "Equī celeriter _____." (to go)

4. Cisium tabellārium celeriter _____. (to carry)

5. Aurēlia, "Syrus," inquit, "celeriter _____ quod tū, Gāī, celeriter iter facere

   _____." (to go) (to wish/want)

Activity 17i Imperatives of Irregular Verbs

Translate the following commands into Latin, using irregular verbs:

1. Carry the trunk to the field, Sextus!

   _____

2. Go to the fields, boys!

   _____

3. Don't hit Cornelia with the ball, Sextus!

   _____

4. Bring the ball, boys!

   _____

5. Go to (your) mother, Cornelia!

   _____

6. Don't play there, boys!

   _____

7. Go to the carriage now, Sextus and Marcus!

   _____

Applying What You Have Learned

Activity 17j Writing the Language

Translate the following English sentences into Latin. Include all long marks. Use the stories and vocabulary lists in your textbook, as well as the vocabulary lists in this book, to help you:

1. The carriage driver was unhappy because he was alone in the road.

   _____

2. Syrus says, "I wanted to avoid the light two-wheeled carriage but was not able."

   _____

3. All the Cornelii and Sextus and Eucleides were going to the inn.

   _____

4. They weren't wanting to spend the night on the road.

   _____

5. Syrus says, "I wasn't wanting to go to the inn because Cornelius was angry."

   _____

Activity 17k Expanding Your English Vocabulary

For each italicized English word below, give the related Latin word and below it the meaning of that Latin word. Then complete each sentence by filling in a word at the right:

Latin Word
Meaning of the Latin Word   **If you ...**

1. _____   describe a skyscraper as an
                            imposing *edifice*, you are saying
   _____   that it is a spectacular   _____

2. _____   are a *custodian* of property,
                            you _____ it.
   _____   _____

3. _____   are drilling in the earth for an
                            aquifer, you are trying to find rock
   _____   or sand that   _____

   _____

   _____

4. _____ you work as a *volunteer*, you do so
   not because you must but because
   _____ you _____ to. _____

5. _____ are looking for the *exit*, you are
   intending to
   _____   _____

Activity 17l Reading Latin

Look at the new vocabulary beneath this story. Then read the story, noting forms of the irregular verbs volō, nōlō, ferō, *and* eō. *Reread the Latin for comprehension. Then mark whether each statement following the story is* V = Vērum *or* F = Falsum:

Aurelia Is Worried, but Sextus Is Not

Dum Cornēliī per viam ad caupōnam ībant, Aurēlia sollicita erat. "Ego pernoctāre in caupōnā nōlō," inquit māter misera, "quod caupōnae semper sunt perīculōsae. Saepe praedōnēs scelestī in caupōnīs pernoctant."

Sextus, quī ad caupōnam īre volēbat, "Fortasse," inquit, "praedōnēs scelestī in caupōnā nostrā sunt! Praedōnēs vidēre volō." Nunc Cornēlia misera lacrimābat quod praedōnēs timēbat.

"Tacē, Sexte! Nolumus fēminās terrēre," inquit Mārcus. Sextus, "Nōlī," inquit, "mē vexāre, Mārce! Omnēs praedōnēs pūgiōnēs et magna bacula sēcum ferunt sed nōs nōn ferimus. Ēheu! Neque baculum neque pūgiōnem ferō sed pilam tantum habeō. Fertne Cornēlius pūgiōnem?"

"Tempus est tacēre, moleste!" inquit Cornēlius, īrā commōtus. "Vīsne terrēre Aurēliam et Cornēliam?"

"Cūr Aurēlia et Cornēlia perterritae sunt?" rogābat puer fatuus.

Nēmō respondēre poterat sed omnēs ad caupōnam celeriter ībant quod advesperāscēbat. Brevī tempore Sextus laetus, "Syrus," inquit, "virgam habet. Praedōnēs virgā Syrī feriam. Syre, ubi es?" "Syrus," inquit Cornēlius, "ad raedam manet." Sextus nōn iam laetus erat.

praedō, praedōnis, m., *robber*
pūgiō, pūgiōnis, m., *knife, dagger*
sēcum, *with them*
feriam, *I will hit*

1. Aurēlia in caupōnīs pernoctāre nōlēbat quod sunt perīculōsae.　　　V　F

2. Sextus praedōnēs in caupōnā vidēre nōlēbat.　　　V　F

3. Mārcus Cornēliam et Aurēliam terrēre volēbat.　　　V　F

4. Sextus neque baculum neque pilam ferēbat.　　　V　F

5. Dum advesperāscēbat, Cornēliī ad caupōnam celeriter ībant.　　　V　F

6. Sextus praedōnēs virgā Syrī feriēbat.　　　V　F

ARRIVAL AT THE INN

> In addition to vocabulary and the story, the activities in this chapter focus on:
> 1. forms of adjectives.
> 2. agreement of nouns and adjectives.

Vocabulary

Activity 18a Vocabulary

Study the vocabulary list on pages 237–238 alone or with a partner. Note that all 3rd declension adjectives you have seen so far are listed.

The Story

Activity 18b Vocabulary in Context

Fill in the blanks with Latin words to match the English cues:

1. _____ obēsus _____ et canēs revocāvit. (A man)
   (appeared)

2. "Hī canes caudās movent _____," inquit Cornēlia, "quod laetī sunt."
   (only)

3. "Nōlīte _____!" (flee)

4. Puella sōla ad canēs _____ extendit. (hand)

5. "_____ hīc in caupōnā," inquit caupō, "_____ prīncipis
   pernoctāvit." (Once) (an envoy)

6. Aurēlia mussat, "Doleō quod in caupōnā _____ necesse est."
   (to spend the night)

7. "_____ _____, caupō est meus amīcus Apollodōrus!"
   inquit Eucleidēs. (Unless I am mistaken)

8. "_____ _____, mī Apollodōre?" (How are you?)

Forms

Adjectives: 1st/2nd Declension and 3rd Declension

Activity 18c Practice with Forms of Adjectives

Supply the proper form of **omnis, -is, -e** *before each of the following nouns and the proper form of* **noster, nostra, nostrum** *after each noun. Be sure to make the adjectives agree with the nouns in gender, case, and number. The words used are in the word bank on the next page:*

	omnis, -is, -e		noster, nostra, nostrum
1.	_____	vīllam	_____
2.	_____	artēs (nom. pl.)	_____
3.	_____	lēgātō	_____
4.	_____	plaustrum	_____
5.	_____	onere	_____
6.	_____	lēgātus	_____
7.	_____	caudae (gen. sing.)	_____
8.	_____	hominem	_____
9.	_____	caudīs	_____
10.	_____	artem	_____
11.	_____	hominibus	_____
12.	_____	plaustra	_____
13.	_____	cauda	_____
14.	_____	onerum	_____
15.	_____	oneris	_____
16.	_____	hominum	_____
17.	_____	plaustrī	_____
18.	_____	arte	_____
19.	_____	caudārum	_____
20.	_____	onera	_____

1st Declension	2nd Declension	3rd Declension
vīlla, -ae, f.	lēgātus, -ī, m.	homō, hominis, m.
cauda, -ae, f.	plaustrum, -ī, n.	ars, artis, f.
		onus, oneris, n.

Building the Meaning

Nouns and Adjectives: Agreement II

Activity 18d Adjective Agreement

Circle the adjective that agrees with the boldface noun in each sentence:

1. **Raeda** in fossā manet (immōbilis / immōbile).

2. Eucleidēs Cornēlium ad **caupōnam** (vīcīnam / vīcīnum) dūcit.

3. **Puerī** (temerārius / temerāriī) ad caupōnam currunt.

4. **Aurēlia et Cornēlia** (sollicitī / sollicitae) lentē ambulant.

5. (Omnis / Omnēs) **Cornēliī** ad caupōnam adveniunt et canēs vident.

6. Ubi canēs lātrant, Sextus, **puer** (ignāvō / ignāvus), fugit.

7. Mārcus tamen nōn est ignāvus; **puer** stat (immōbilis / immōbilibus).

8. Cornēlia est **puella** (forte / fortis) et manum extendit.

9. Tum **homō** (obēsus / obēsō) appāruit.

10. Eucleidēs **caupōnem** (obēsam / obēsum) salūtat quod agnōscit amīcum.

What Noun Does an Adjective Modify?
How Do You Decide?

Activity 18e What Noun Does the Adjective Modify?

Consider the gender, case, and number of each adjective to determine what noun it modifies. Then translate each sentence:

1. Caupō bonum amīcum habet. _____

2. Bonus amīcus est servus. _____

3. Dominus bonī servī est Cornēlius. _____

4. Caupōna bonī caupōnis est vīcīna. _____

5. Servus bonum caupōnem salūtat. _____

6. Caupō bonus amīcum salūtat. _____

7. Caupō bonō cum servō sedet. _____

8. Servus bonō cum caupōne sedet. _____

9. Puella fortis ad canēs manum extendit. _____

10. Canēs fortem puellam salūtant. _____

11. Puella fortibus cum canibus lūdit. _____

12. Canēs fortī cum puellā lūdunt. _____

13. Puella est amīca fortium canum. _____

14. Canēs sunt amīcī fortis puellae. _____

Applying What You Have Learned

Activity 18f Writing the Language

Translate the following English sentences into Latin. Include all long marks. Use the stories and vocabulary lists in your textbook, as well as the vocabulary lists in this book, to help you:

1. Aurelia was going toward the nearby inn slowly because she did not want to spend the night there.

   _____

   _____

2. Suddenly the rash dogs bark fiercely and make for the Cornelii.

   _____

   _____

3. Cornelia holds out her hand to the big dogs, and the dogs wag their tails.

   _____

   _____

4. At that very moment a fat man appears at the door of the inn and greets the tired guests.

_____

_____

5. Eucleides happily (use adjective, not adverb) shouts, "I recognize my friend Apollodorus!"

_____

_____

6. The Greek innkeeper replies, "I am glad that you are coming to my inn. Come in, everyone!"

_____

_____

Activity 18g Expanding Your English Vocabulary

Using the word bank below, write the word that could replace the italicized word or words in each sentence. Use the Latin words in parentheses to help determine the meaning of the English words. Then write the English translation of each Latin word in the word bank:

1. Aurelia thinks Cornelius's decision was too *rushed*.   _____

2. Cornelia shows great *courage* with the dogs.   _____

3. In the courtyard of the inn, we could see *dog-like* tracks.   _____

4. Did an *official representative* of the emperor stay at this inn?   _____

5. Aurelia thinks it was a *mistake* to stay at the inn.   _____

6. Aurelia prays to the *all-powerful* gods for help.   _____

7. Cornelius's decision is *unable to be called back*.   _____

8. Syrus *handles* the reins with great skill.   _____

9. Because the printing press had not been invented, all writing in the ancient world had to be done *by hand*.   _____

10. Cornelius sees the inn as a *place to retreat to for safety*.   _____

11. With a *sad* sigh, Aurelia reluctantly follows Cornelius.   _____

refuge (**fugere**) _____	omnipotent (**omnis**) _____ (+ **posse**, *to be able*)
irrevocable (**revocāre**) _____	fortitude (**fortis**) _____
precipitate (**sē praecipitant**) _____	legate (**lēgātus**) _____
manually (**manum**) _____	doleful (**dolēre**) _____
manipulates (**manum**) _____	error (**errō**) _____
canine (**canēs**) _____	

Activity 18h Reading Latin

Look at the new vocabulary on the next page. Then read the story, noting agreement of adjectives and nouns. Reread the story for comprehension. Then answer the questions on the next page with complete Latin sentences:

Uncle Titus

Intereā, in urbe Rōmā frāter Cornēliī, nōmine Titus, in hortō sedēbat. Multī servī fortēs et ancillae strēnuae labōrābant, sed Titus prope piscīnam vīcīnam sedēbat et amīcōs cārōs exspectābat. Nōn labōrābat. Neque epistulās scrībēbat neque legēbat. Nihil facere solēbat. Titus omnibus cum amīcīs cēnāre et in lectō dormīre modo volēbat.

Tum vōcēs hominum procul audit. Titus sibi, "Nisi errō," inquit, "vōcēs amīcōrum fidēlium meōrum audiō."

Duo hominēs brevēs et obēsī intrant et Titum salūtant. "Salvē, noster Tite! Tempus est breve! Tempus est cēnāre!"

"Salvēte, amīcī meī," repondet Titus. "Laetus vōs videō. Servī meī cēnam nōbīs parāvērunt."

"Quālem cibum parāvērunt?"

"Porcum suāvem et ingentem parāvērunt!" Trēs amicī igitur celeriter trīclīnium ēlegāns intrant et in lectīs accumbunt. Titus, "Sollicitus et vexātus sum," inquit. "Hodiē enim ad Portam Capēnam iī quod meus frāter Cornēlius, vir gravis, cum uxōre et līberīs ad urbem redīre in animō habēbat. Diū ad portam sedēbam et exspectābam sed nōn advēnit. Cornēlius est senātor nōbilis sed homō tardus."

"Quid accidit? Suntne omnēs incolumēs?" rogat amīcus Titī.

"Nesciō. Crās iterum ad portam mihi redīre necesse erit. Ecce! Meī servī cibum ferunt! Nostra cēna advenit. Servī meī tardī nōn sunt!"

cārus, -a, -um, *dear, beloved*

cēnō, cēnāre, *to eat dinner*

sibi, *to himself*

fidēlis, -is, -e, *faithful*

cēna, -ae, f., *dinner*

parāvērunt, (*they*) *have prepared*

porcus, -ī, m., *pig*

suāvis, -is, -e, *sweet, delightful*

ingēns, ingentis, *huge*

trīclīnium, -ī, n., *dining room*

ēlegāns, ēlegantis, *elegant*

lectus, -ī, m., *couch*

accumbō, accumbere, *to lie down, recline*

vexātus, -a, -um, *annoyed*

iī, *I went*

gravis, -is, -e, *serious*

advēnit, *he did come*

nōbilis, -is, -e, *noble*

accidit, *happened*

erit, *it will be*

1. Quot et quālēs servōs et ancillās habet Titus?

_____

2. Quālēs hominēs Titum salūtant?

_____

3. Quālem porcum parāvērunt servī Titī?

_____

4. Quāle trīclīnium habet Titus?

_____

5. Quālem frātrem habet Titus?

_____

SETTLING IN

In addition to vocabulary and the story, the activities in this chapter focus on:
1. perfect tense endings of verbs (3rd person singular and plural).
2. perfect stems of verbs.
3. translating the perfect tense.
4. identifying the tense of verbs.

Vocabulary

Activity 19a Vocabulary

Study the vocabulary list on pages 239–240 alone or with a partner. Go to the corresponding list on the Companion website where you will find verbs for review with their perfect tense forms.

The Story

Activity 19b Vocabulary in Context

Fill in the blanks with Latin words to match the English cues:

1. "_____ mē ad cubiculum meum!" (Take . . . !)

2. Aurēlia est _____ dēfessa. (very)

3. Aurēlia et Cornēlia cubiculum _____ sed lectus erat

   _____. (entered) (dirty)

4. Ubi Apollodōrus _____ _____ temptāvit, Eucleidēs
   eum reprehendit. (to explain the situation)

5. "Nōn necesse est _____ mē reprehendere," inquit caupō. (for you, *sing.*)

6. Servī alium _____ parant. (bed)

7. "Hic lectus est _____," inquit Aurēlia. (better)

8. Aurēlia dēfessa _____ _____ vult. (to go to bed)

9. Aurēlia et Cornēlia cubitum _____. (went)

10. Aurēlia mox dormiēbat, sed Cornēlia dormīre nōn poterat et _____.
    (was staying awake)

11. Puerī _____ volunt quod ēsuriunt. (to dine)

12. Caupō servōs _____ cēnam Cornēliō et Mārcō et Sextō parāre. (ordered)

13. Servī bonam _____ Cornēliō et Mārcō et Sextō parāvērunt. (dinner)

14. Cornēlius, "Necesse est _____, puerī," inquit, "mox cubitum īre." (for you)

Forms

Verbs: Perfect Tense I

Activity 19c Perfect Tense Forms

Write the missing forms of each verb in the proper columns. The first set is done for you:

Present 3rd Sing.	Present 3rd Pl.	Perfect 3rd Sing.	Perfect 3rd Pl.
1. intrat	*intrant*	*intrāvit*	intrāvērunt
2. _____	iubent	iussit	_____
3. dūcit	_____	dūxit	_____
4. _____	gemunt	_____	gemuērunt
5. videt	_____	_____	vīdērunt
6. _____	explicant	explicāvit	_____
7. advenit	_____	advēnit	_____

Activity 19d Perfect Stems, Perfect Endings, and Translating Verbs in the Perfect Tense

Put a box around the stem of each perfect tense verb at the left and then change singular forms to plural and plural forms to singular. Translate the resulting verb three different ways, following the example:

1. ⬚intrāv⬚it   *intrāvērunt*   *they entered*   *they have entered*   *they did enter*

2. iussērunt   _____   _____   _____   _____

3. gemuit   _____   _____   _____   _____

4. dūxērunt   _____   _____   _____   _____

5. advēnērunt   _____   _____   _____   _____

6. mussāvit   _____   _____   _____   _____

7. timuērunt   _____   _____   _____   _____

8. verberāvit   _____   _____   _____   _____

9. arripuērunt   _____   _____   _____   _____

10. vīdit   _____   _____   _____   _____

Activity 19e Identifying Tenses

Underline all verbs in the present tense, put a box around all verbs in the imperfect tense, and circle all verbs in the perfect tense. Then translate the sentences:

1. Trēs viātōrēs caupōnam Apollodōrī intrāvērunt et rogāvērunt, "Habēsne cubiculum nōbīs?"

_____

2. "Certē," respondit caupō Graecus, "est in meā caupōnā bonum cubiculum vōbīs."

_____

3. Statim servī cubiculum pūrgāvērunt et trēs lectōs in cubiculum mōvērunt.

_____

4. Intereā in culīna ancillae magnam cēnam parābant.

_____

5. Caupō dēfessus quoque strēnuē labōrābat.

_____

6. Viātōrēs in caupōnā sedēbant.

_____

7. Mox cēnāvērunt quod valdē ēsuriēbant.

_____

8. Advesperāscēbat et canēs caupōnis obēsī lātrābant.

_____

9. Cūnctae ancillae clāmāvērunt, "Aliī viātōrēs ad caupōnam adveniunt!" Tum gemuērunt quod dēfessae erant.

_____

_____

10. Apollodōrus sēmisomnus iānuam iterum aperuit et clāmāvit, "Salvēte, viātōrēs!"

_____

_____

Applying What You Have Learned

Activity 19f Writing the Language

Translate the following English sentences into Latin. Include all long marks. Use the stories and vocabulary lists in your textbook, as well as the vocabulary lists in this book, to help you:

1. Cornelius was worried because all inns were dangerous and many innkeepers were wicked.

_____

2. He entered the large inn, however, and ordered the fat innkeeper to prepare a good dinner.

_____

3. Cornelius dined with all the travelers.

_____

4. Suddenly Aurelia groaned because the bedroom was dirty.

_____

5. Soon the slaves of the innkeeper carried a better bed into the bedroom.

_____

6. Cornelius's tired wife was able to go to bed.

_____

Activity 19g Expanding Your English Vocabulary

For each italicized English word below, give the related Latin word (for verbs, give the infinitive) and below it the meaning of that Latin word. Then complete each sentence by filling in a word at the right:

Latin Word
Meaning of the Latin Word   **If you …**

1. _____   complain *vehemently*,
                                you complain very

   _____   _____

2. _____   reveal a *sordid* secret, you
                                reveal something that is

   _____   _____

3. _____   offer *explication* of a difficult
                                problem, you provide an

   _____   _____

4. _____   try to *ameliorate* a difficult
                                situation, you try to make it

   _____   _____

5. _____   keep a *vigilant* eye on your
                                belongings, you are being
                                _____ over them.

   _____   _____

6. _____   speak *explicitly*, you explain
                                things very

   _____   _____

7. _____   *certify* something, you declare
                                it to be accurate, true, and

   _____   _____

8. _____   maintain an all-night *vigil*, you
                                 _____ until dawn.   _____

_____

9. _____   join a *vigilante* group, you
                                 join a group that keeps _____   _____
                                 over the security of the
_____   community by taking the law
                                 into its own hands.

10. _____   are looking with *esurient*
                                 eyes, your look is   _____

_____

Activity 19h Reading Latin

Look at the new vocabulary on the next page. Then read the story, noting verbs in the perfect tense. Reread the story for comprehension. Then mark whether each statement following the story is V = Vērum (true) or F = Falsum (false):

Not Quite Ready to Sleep

Ubi Cornēliī ad caupōnam advēnērunt, Aurēlia intrāre nōluit quod timuit.

Fīliam tamen per iānuam dūxit. Cornēlia cēnāre valdē volēbat, sed eī nōn licuit

quod māter, "Nōs hīc," inquit, "cēnāre nōn possumus."

Mox caupō mātrem et fīliam ad cubiculum dūxit. Cubiculum sordidum erat!

Lectus erat sordidus, et erat pulvis undique. Sub alterō lectō fēlem obēsam vīdit

Cornēlia. Dum caupō et māter Cornēliae dē lectō clāmābant, puella laeta ad

fēlem manum extendēbat. Fēlēs tamen ē cubiculō cucurrit. Cornēlia gemuit.

Aurēlia iussit caupōnem novum lectum parāre. Servī caupōnis alium lectum

in cubiculum portāvērunt et Aurēlia et Cornēlia statim cubitum iērunt. Māter

obdormīvit, sed fīlia vigilābat quod vōcēs et clāmōrēs procul audīvit. "Suntne

vōcēs puerōrum? Vigilatne adhūc pater? Quālēs hominēs adsunt in caupōnā?"

Puella cūriōsa tacitē surrēxit.

eī nōn licuit, *she was not allowed*
undique, adv., *everywhere*
fēlēs, fēlis, gen. pl., **fēlium,** f., *cat*
obdormiō, obdormīre, *to go to sleep*
adsum, adesse, *to be present*
cūriōsus, -a, -um, *curious*
surrēxit, *(she) arose*

1. Cornēlia et Aurēlia caupōnam intrāvērunt.   V   F

2. Māter et fīlia ad cubiculum cum caupōne iērunt.   V   F

3. Fēlēs Cornēliam sub lectō vīdit.   V   F

4. Cornēlia laeta erat quod fēlēs fūgit.   V   F

5. Cornēlia et Aurēlia surrēxērunt quod vōcēs et clāmōrēs audīvērunt.   V   F

CHANCE ENCOUNTER

> *In addition to vocabulary and the story, the activities in this chapter focus on:*
> 1. the perfect tense of verbs (all persons and numbers).
> 2. subordinate clauses with the conjunction **dum**.
> 3. uses of the infinitive.
> 4. principal parts of verbs.

Vocabulary

Activity 20a Vocabulary

Study the vocabulary list on page 241 alone or with a partner. Go to the corresponding list on the Companion website where you will find lists of coordinating and subordinating conjunctions and a list of verbs with their principal parts for review.

The Story

Activity 20b Vocabulary in Context

Fill in the blanks with Latin words to match the English cues:

1. Aurēlia et Cornēlia cubitum iērunt, sed Mārcus et Sextus cum Cornēliō

   _____. (stayed)

2. _____ cēnam ad _____ _____ vigilāre in animō habuērunt.
   (After) (midnight)

3. Mārcus et Sextus ēsuriunt et Mārcus patrem rogat, "_____ _____ hīc
   cēnāre?" (May we)

4. _____ tacēbat pater, tandem, "Estō!" inquit. (For a short time)

5. Rīsērunt puerī quod laetī erant. Voluērunt _____ ibi cēnāre et aliōs
   viātōrēs spectāre. (for)

6. "Gaudēmus, pater," inquit Mārcus, "quod nōs in cubiculum nōn statim

   _____." (you have sent)

7. "_____ enim omnia vidēre et audīre." (We wanted)

8. Dum puerī cibum _____ dēvorant, subitō intrāvit _____
   quīdam. (very good) (soldier)

9. "Cūr vōs _____ _____ _____
intrāvistis?" (into this inn)

10. "Cūr hoc nōbīs _____?" rogāvit Cornēlius. (are you saying)

11. "In agrīs nocte manēre nōlēbāmus, sed _____ _____ in
caupōnā pernoctāvimus." (never before)

12. "Audīvī _____ _____ dē caupōne quī hospitem

_____." (story) (told) (killed)

13. "Volō illam fābulam dē caupōne _____." (to tell)

14. "Nōbīs illam fābulam _____, mīles!" inquit Cornēlius. (tell!)

Forms

Verbs: Perfect Tense II

Activity 20c Perfect Stems and Endings

Circle the perfect stem in the 3rd principal part of the following verbs and then fill in the correct perfect tense forms to go with the pronouns and nouns:

maneō, manēre, mānsī, mānsus

nōs _____   puellae _____

puella _____   vōs _____

ego _____   tū _____

dormiō, dormīre, dormīvī, dormītūrus

puerī _____   tū _____

puer _____   ego _____

nōs _____   vōs _____

Building the Meaning

Subordinate Clauses with the Conjunction *dum*

Activity 20d Subordinate Clauses with the Conjunction *dum*

Underline all verbs in the present tense, put a box around all verbs in the imperfect tense, and circle all verbs in the perfect tense. Then translate the sentences:

1. Dum canēs lātrant, caupō appāruit.

_____

2. Dum Cornēliī in caupōnam intrābant, Syrus cum raedā et equīs manēbat.

_____

3. Servī cēnam parābant, dum puerī in caupōnā sedēbant.

_____

4. Dum puerī cēnam dēvorant, mīles intrāvit.

_____

5. Dum puerī cēnant, Cornēlia in cubiculō cum mātre manet.

_____

6. Dum Aurēlia dormit, Cornēlia ē cubiculō exiit.

_____

Uses of the Infinitive

Activity 20e Uses of the Infinitive

Underline the infinitives in the following sentences and put boxes around the verbs or phrases with which each infinitive is used. Identify the use of each infinitive from the choices provided below by writing the appropriate letter in the slot. Then translate the sentences:

Uses of infinitives:

    a. Complementary infinitive
    b. Infinitive with impersonal verb or verbal phrase
    c. Infinitive subject of the verb **est**
    d. Accusative and infinitive with verbs such as **docēre** or **iubēre**

1. Intrāre in caupōnam perīculōsum est.

_____

Use of Infinitive: _____

2. Aurēlia ibi manēre nōn vult.

_____

Use of Infinitive: _____

3. Cornēlia sedēre cum puerīs et fābulās audīre voluit.

_____

Use of Infinitive: _____

4. Sed necesse erat manēre cum mātre in cubiculō.

_____

Use of Infinitive: _____

5. "Nōn licet tibi, Cornēlia," Aurēlia inquit, "in caupōnā sedēre et cēnāre."

_____

Use of Infinitive: _____

6. Semper Aurēlia docet Cornēliam esse bonam puellam.

_____

Use of Infinitive: _____

Verbs: Principal Parts

Activity 20f Principal Parts That Follow Set Patterns

Give the 2nd, 3rd, and 4th principal parts of these verbs that follow set patterns:

1. parō _____   _____   _____

2. habeō _____   _____   _____

3. audiō _____   _____   _____

Activity 20g Principal Parts of Irregular Verbs

Give the 2nd, 3rd, and 4th principal parts of these irregular verbs:

1. sum _____   _____   _____

2. eō _____   _____ or _____   _____

Activity 20h Principal Parts and the Perfect Tense

Using the two forms that are given, deduce and give the first three principal parts for each verb (note that 3rd conjugation -iō verbs are identified):

	Present, 1st Sing.	Infinitive	Perfect, 1st Sing.
1. rīdēs, rīsistī	_____	_____	_____
2. faciunt, fēcērunt (3rd -iō)	_____	_____	_____
3. cadimus, cecidimus	_____	_____	_____

	Present, 1st Sing.	Infinitive	Perfect, 1st Sing.
4. stātis, stetistis	_____	_____	_____
5. venīs, vēnistī	_____	_____	_____
6. dīcunt, dīxērunt	_____	_____	_____
7. concidimus, concidimus	_____	_____	_____
8. fugiunt, fūgērunt (3rd *-iō*)	_____	_____	_____
9. ascendit, ascendit	_____	_____	_____
10. pōnitis, posuistis	_____	_____	_____

Activity 20i Present, Imperfect, and Perfect

Fill in the corresponding forms for the missing tenses. Keep the same person and number. Note that these are the same verbs as the ones in Activitiy 20h, for which you deduced the principal parts. The first one is done for you:

Present	Imperfect	Perfect
1. rīdētis	*rīdēbātis*	*rīsistis*
2. _____	faciēbam	_____
3. _____	_____	cecidistī
4. stant	_____	_____
5. _____	veniēbat	_____
6. dīcis	_____	_____
7. conciditis	_____	_____
8. _____	fugiēbās	_____
9. _____	_____	ascendī
10. _____	pōnēbās	_____

Applying What You Have Learned

Activity 20j Writing the Language

Translate the following English sentences into Latin. Include all long marks. Use the stories and vocabulary lists in your textbook, as well as the vocabulary lists in this book, to help you:

1. When did you go to bed, Aurelia and Cornelia?

   _____

2. We have prepared a very good dinner for you, Cornelius.

   _____

3. While Cornelius and the boys were eating dinner, a soldier came to the inn.

   _____

4. We have never heard that story told about an innkeeper.

   _____

5. To sleep in the inn was not dangerous.

   _____

Activity 20k Expanding Your English Vocabulary

Using the word bank on the next page, write the word that could replace the italicized word or words in each sentence. Use the Latin words in parentheses to help determine the meaning of the English words. Then write the English translation of each Latin word in the word bank:

1. By his accent and *choice of words*, Cornelius can tell that the soldier comes from the northern provinces.   _____

2. Romans built large tombs in order to leave an impressive legacy to *those who would be born after them*.   _____

3. The empire is maintained through *the army's* might.   _____

4. Aurelia was not afraid to *speak against* Cornelius's plan.   _____

5. The inn does not provide *the best* accommodations.   _____

6. Eucleides always has a *story with a moral lesson* to tell the boys.   _____

7. Who could have *foretold* their misfortune on the road?   _____

8. The scene was *wonderful*, like those described in fairy tales. _____

9. The soldier is a dramatic *storyteller*. _____

10. Cornelius will be the *one who finds middle ground* in the
dispute in the Senate. _____

posterity (**post**) _____	diction (**dīcere**) _____
contradict (**contrā**, *against*) +	narrator (**nārrāre**) _____
(**dīcere**) _____	predicted (**prae-**, *before*) +
fabulous (**fābula**) _____	(**dīcere**) _____
mediator (**medius**) _____	military (**mīles**) _____
optimal (**optimus**) _____	fable (**fābula**) _____

Activity 20I Reading Latin

*Look at the new vocabulary following this story. Then read the story, noting **dum** clauses, uses of infinitives, and verbs in the perfect tense (1st, 2nd, and 3rd person). Reread the story for comprehension. Then rewrite the sentences below, correcting the factual errors in them based on the information in the story:*

What a Snore!

Dum raeda in fossā haerēbat immōbilis, Syrus sōlus in viā manēbat; necesse

enim erat raedam et equōs custōdīre. "Ēheu!" gemuit raedārius. "Nōn licet mihi

in caupōnā pernoctāre quod raedam ē fossā extrahere nōn potuī. Perīculōsum est

hīc pernoctāre. Ō mē miserum!" Dum equī sub arboribus post raedam quiēscunt,

obdormīvit in raedā Syrus.

Mediā nocte trēs praedōnēs per Viam Appiam tacitē ambulābant. Rogāvit

ūnus praedō, "Quid in caupōnā vīdistis?"

"Senātōrem Rōmānum in caupōnā cōnspeximus, sed cum mīlite sedēbat,"

respondit alius praedō. "Caupō nōs discēdere iussit. Quid in viā vīdistī tū?"

"In viā nihil vīdī."

"Ecce!" interpellāvit tertius praedō. "Vidētisne raedam?"

Deinde cistās in agrō cōnspexērunt. Ad eās statim appropinquāvērunt et vestēs extraxērunt. Subitō stertuit in raedā raedārius. Praedōnēs timēbant, nam Syrum vidēre nōn potuērunt. Celeriter aufūgērunt et vestēs in agrō relīquērunt.

Prīmā lūce raedārius surrēxit. "Quam dēfessus eram! Mehercule! Cūr vestēs in agrō sunt?" exclāmāvit. Circumspexit in omnēs partēs, sed nihil vīdit. Itaque vestēs in cistās iterum posuit.

possum, posse, potuī, *to be able*
post, prep. + acc., *after, behind*
obdormiō, -īre, -īvī, -ītūrus, *to go to sleep*
praedō, praedōnis, m., *robber*
cōnspiciō, cōnspicere, cōnspexī, cōnspectus, *to catch sight of*
tertius, -a, -um, *third*
vestis, vestis, gen. pl., **vestium,** f., *clothes*
stertō, stertere, stertuī, *to snore*
aufugiō, aufugere, aufūgī, *to run away*
surgō, surgere, surrēxī, surrēctūrus, *to get up, rise*
circumspiciō, circumspicere, circumspexī, circumspectus, *to look around*

1. Praedōnēs in viā pernoctābant quod raedam extrahere nōn potuērunt.

_____

2. Servus sub arboribus post raedam dormīvit.

_____

3. Ūnus praedō, "Quid in caupōnā vīdī?" rogāvit.

_____

4. Alius praedō, "Senātōrem Rōmānum in caupōnā vīdī," inquit.

_____

5. Syrus exclāmāvit, "Quam dēfessus erās!"

_____

MURDER

In addition to vocabulary and the story, the activities in this chapter focus on:
1. principal parts of verbs.
2. verbs.

Vocabulary

Activity 21a Vocabulary

Study the vocabulary list on pages 242–243 alone or with a partner. Go to the corresponding list on the Companion website where you will find a list of verbs for review and a list of verbs grouped by their perfect stem markers.

The Story

Activity 21b Vocabulary in Context

Fill in the blanks with Latin words to match the English cues:

1. Aurēlia _____ caupōnam intrāvit. (unwilling(ly))

2. Īrāta erat ubi lectum sordidum _____. (saw)

3. Caupō tamen servōs _____ alium lectum in cubiculum movēre et cēnam nōbīs parāre. (ordered)

4. Postquam cēnam _____ mīles fābulam nārrāvit. (we finished)

5. Dum Septimus dormit, Aulus eī in _____ appāruit. (sleep)

6. "Necesse est tibi," inquit Aulus, "ad caupōnam _____ īre." (in the morning)

7. "Meum _____ _____ valdē timeō," _____ Septimus. (dream) (bad) (thought)

8. Septimus _____ _____ nōn poterat. (to wake up)

9. Caupō _____ Aulī in plaustrum posuit et stercus _____ iēcit. (body) (on top)

10. Septimus ad caupōnam _____ _____ iit. (at dawn)

11. Caupō _____ scelestus vidētur. (to him)

12. Septimus Aulum _____ sub stercore _____. (dead)
    (found)

13. Cīvēs caupōnem, quamquam innocentiam _____, _____.
    (he was pretending) (punished)

14. Puerī gaudēbant, quod _____ cubitum īre licēbat. (late)

Verbs

Activity 21c Principal Parts

Fill in the missing principal parts and write the conjugation numbers or irreg. *for irregular verb on the lines at the right:*

1. _____ _____ posuī _____ _____

2. _____ _____ _____ surrēctūrus _____

3. _____ removēre _____ _____ _____

4. inveniō _____ _____ _____ _____

5. _____ _____ iussī _____ _____

6. _____ _____ _____ adiūtus _____

7. _____ _____ iī _____ _____

8. dīcō _____ _____ _____ _____

9. _____ _____ petīvī _____ _____

10. _____ _____ nōluī _____ _____

11. _____ esse _____ _____ _____

12. _____ _____ _____ vīsus _____

13. _____ respondēre _____ _____ _____

14. possum _____ _____ _____ _____

15. _____ _____ _____ coniectus _____

16. _____ relinquere _____ _____ _____

17. _____ velle _____ _____ _____

18. _____ _____ tremuī _____ _____

19. extrahō _____ _____ _____ _____

20. _____ _____ sēdī _____ _____

21. _____ effugere _____ _____ _____

22. rīdeō _____ _____ _____ _____

Activity 21d Finding the Verb That Does Not Belong

In 1–6, one verb does not belong because it is not the same tense as the others. Circle the verb that does not belong. The first set is done for you:

1. (adiuvant)   amāvērunt   iussērunt   vēnērunt

2. portāvērunt   sunt   removēmus   dormīmus

3. poterās   erāmus   faciēbās   extrahimus

4. adiūvērunt   fuit   dīximus   invenītis

5. pūniēbat   poterat   est   clāmābat

6. habuistis   cōgitātis   pūnītis   timētis

In 7–12, one verb does not belong because it is not the same person and number as the others. Circle the verb that does not belong. The first set is done for you:

7. adiūvī   taceō   (erāmus)   exclāmō

8. poteram   eō   parāvistī   posuī

9. es   appāruī   iussistī   lacrimās

10. facimus   iēcimus   agitis   sedēmus

11. sum   necāvī   ībam   vīdistī

12. nōn vīs   appropinquāvistī   poterat   erās

Activity 21e Translating Verbs

Match each verb with its correct translation:

1. iaciunt	_____	**a.** they have thrown
2. removet	_____	**b.** we kept throwing
3. mīsimus	_____	**c.** we are sending
4. removēbant	_____	**d.** they are throwing
5. iēcistī	_____	**e.** I did remove
6. remōvit	_____	**f.** he does remove
7. mittitis	_____	**g.** we were sending
8. removeō	_____	**h.** you do send
9. iaciēbāmus	_____	**i.** they were removing
10. mittēbās	_____	**j.** you were throwing
11. iēcērunt	_____	**k.** we have sent
12. mittimus	_____	**l.** you kept sending
13. remōvī	_____	**m.** you threw
14. mittēbāmus	_____	**n.** I remove
15. iaciēbās	_____	**o.** she removed

Activity 21f Making and Translating Perfect Tense Forms

Circle the subjects in the sentences below. Then fill in the blank with the correct form of the verb in parentheses in the perfect tense. Finally, translate each sentence:

1. Puerī _____, "Ubi tū, mīles, hanc fābulam _____?"
(rogāre) (audīre)

_____

2. "Amīcus," mīles _____, "hanc fābulam mihi _____."
(respondēre) (nārrāre)

_____

3. Duo amīcī, Aulus et Septimus, ōlim in Graeciā iter _____. (facere)

_____

4. Septimus in vīllā hospitis _____, sed Aulus _____ ad caupōnam. (pernoctāre) (īre)

_____

5. Aulus Septimō in somnō _____ et, "Adiuvā mē!" inquit. (appārēre)

_____

6. Septimus _____ sed mox iterum _____. (surgere) (obdormīre)

_____

7. Aulus iterum Septimō in somnō _____ et "Caupō mē _____

quod tū nōn _____," inquit. (appārēre) (necāre) (venīre)

_____

_____

8. Septimus caupōnem _____. (accūsāre)

_____

9. "Cūr tū," inquit caupō, "mē _____. (accūsāre)

_____

10. Cīvēs caupōnem _____. (pūnīre)

_____

11. Mīles fābulam dē caupōne malō nārrātam _____. (fīnīre)

_____

12. "Tūne _____ hīc anteā?" _____ Mārcus. (pernoctāre) (rogāre)

_____

13. "Minimē," _____ mīles, "sed ego in multīs aliīs caupōnīs

_____." (respondēre) (pernoctāre)

_____

Name _____ Date _____ Period _____

Applying What You Have Learned

Activity 21g Writing the Language

Translate the following English sentences into Latin. Include all long marks. Use the stories and vocabulary lists in your textbook, as well as the vocabulary lists in this book, to help you:

1. Once Aulus made a journey in Greece.

_____

2. He could not find his friend's country house, and so he spent the night in an inn.

_____

3. When the innkeeper saw the tired traveler, he ordered (his) slaves to help him.

_____

4. But that night he killed (his) guest.

_____

5. In the morning he hid the body under the dung in a wagon.

_____

6. The citizens, when they removed the dung and saw Aulus dead, accused the innkeeper and punished (him).

_____

_____

Activity 21h Expanding Your English Vocabulary

For each italicized English word below, give the related Latin word and below it the meaning of that Latin word. Then complete each sentence by filling in a word at the right:

Latin word(s)
Meaning of the Latin Word

If you are ...

1. _____   distributing a *petition*, you are
                               _____ support for a cause.   _____

_____

2. _____ a *somnambulist*, you are a _____

_____

_____

3. _____ receiving *corporal* punishment, _____
you are receiving _____
_____ punishment.

4. _____ *immortal*, you will never
be
_____ _____

5. _____ taking time to *cogitate*, you are
taking time to _____ carefully.
_____ _____

6. _____ a person of *infinite* wisdom,
your wisdom has no
_____

7. _____ making a *deposit*, you are
_____ something aside.
_____ _____

8. _____ *corpulent*, you have a large _____

_____

9. _____ considering *punitive* measures,
you are looking for ways to
_____ _____

10. _____ a general's *adjutant*, you _____
the general.
_____ _____

11. _____ in a *mortuary*, you are in a place
devoted to people who are
_____ _____

12. _____ *simulating* interest, you _____
to be interested.
_____ _____

Activity 21i Reading Latin

Look at the new vocabulary on the next page. Then read the story, noting uses of imperfect and perfect tenses. Reread the story for comprehension. Then match the first parts of the sentences following the story to the clauses that correctly complete them:

A Slave Overnight

Cornēlia in culīnā vīllae stābat sōla. Calceōs nōn habēbat et tunicam sordidam gerēbat. "Venīte, servī! Venīte, ancillae!" clāmābat Cornēlia. "Ubi estis, ignāvī servī? Quid agitis?"

Nēmō vēnit. Iterum iterumque Cornēlia clāmābat, sed nihil nisi silentium erat. Tandem vōcēs servōrum audīvit. Subitō appāruit Dāvus et aliī servī. Brevī tempore circum Cornēliam cōnstitērunt. Omnēs togās gerēbant. Tum Dāvus, "Quid est," inquit, "ancilla?"

Cui Cornēlia, "Nōn tibi licet mē ancillam vocāre."

Respondit Dāvus īrātus, "Servus nōn sum, sed tū ancilla es. Ecce! Ego, ut vidēre potes, togam gerō; tū geris tunicam sordidam. Tū es Syra, serva amīcī meī, Cornēliī."

Stupuit Cornēlia et clāmāvit, "Cornēlia sum, nōn Syra." Sed nēmō eam audiēbat.

Subitō clāmābant servī, "Fer vīnum! Fer cibum! Pūrgā vīllam! Coque cibum! Movē cistam! Nōlī cessāre!"

Hūc illūc currēbat Cornēlia. Tulit cibum et vīnum. Mōvit cistam. Pūrgāvit vīllam, coxit cibum, omnia sōla cūrāvit. Strēnuē labōrābat Cornēlia, quae iam effugere voluit. Tum clāmāvit Dāvus, "Tacēte, omnēs! Appropinquat dominus Syrae!"

Omnēs statim tacuērunt et iānuam spectābant. Intrāvit dominus. Nōn fuit pater Cornēliae. Nōn fuit homō! Vīdit Cornēlia perterrita canem ingentem et exclāmāvit, "Fer mihi auxilium!"

Oculōs aperuit. Aurēlia prope lectum stābat sollicita.

ātrium, -ī, n., *main room*

calceus, -ī, m., *shoe*

circum, prep. + acc, *around*

cōnsistō, cōnsistere, cōnstitī, *to come to a halt, stand still*

pessimus, -a, -um, *very bad, worst*

stupeō, stupēre, stupuī, *to be amazed, gape*

vīnum, -ī, n., *wine*

coquō, coquere, coxī, coctus, *to cook*

oculus, -ī, m., *eye*

1. Dāvus iam togam gerēbat sed Cornēlia _____

2. Cornēlia ancilla fuit sed Dāvus _____

3. Cornēlia effugere voluit quod _____

4. Cornēlia perterrita exclāmāvit _____

5. Cornēlia oculōs aperuit; _____

a. somnium modo fuit.

b. semper strenuē labōrābat.

c. tunicam sordidam gerēbat neque calceōs habēbat.

d. quod dominus fuit canis ingēns.

e. servus nōn fuit.

FROM THE INN TO ROME

In addition to vocabulary and the story, the activities in this chapter focus on:
1. dative singular and plural forms of nouns, adjectives, and pronouns.
2. 3rd declension adjectives of one termination.
3. uses of the dative case.
4. determining whether nouns with identical endings are in the dative or ablative case.

Vocabulary

Activity 22a Vocabulary

Study the vocabulary list on pages 244–245 alone or with a partner.

The Story

Activity 22b Questions about the Story

To whom …? To what …? **Cui …? Quibus …?** Answer the following questions with words in the dative case, keeping to the story in Chapter 22:

1. Cui servī cistās Cornēliōrum trādidērunt? _____

2. Cui Sextus mīlitis fābulam nārrābat? _____

3. Quibus Eucleidēs mandāta dabat? _____

4. Quibus Cornēlius clāmābat? _____

5. Cui Sextus omnia dē mūre mortuō explicāvit? _____

6. Cui Cornēlius mīlitis fābulam nārrāvit? _____

7. Cui appropinquābant Cornēliī? _____

8. Quibus nōn licet intrā urbem sepulcra habēre? _____

9. Cui Mārcus nihil respondit? _____

10. Cui Cornēlius omnia explicāvit? _____

Forms

Nouns: Cases and Declensions: Dative Case

Activity 22c Dative Forms of Nouns by Declension

Write the declension number and the dative singular and plural forms of each of the following nouns. The nominative and genitive singular are supplied:

	Declension	Dative Singular	Dative Plural
1. viātor, viātōris	_____	_____	_____
2. fābula, fābulae	_____	_____	_____
3. ager, agrī	_____	_____	_____
4. auxilium, auxiliī	_____	_____	_____
5. lectus, lectī	_____	_____	_____
6. homō, hominis	_____	_____	_____
7. lēgātus, lēgātī	_____	_____	_____
8. hospes, hospitis	_____	_____	_____
9. vir, virī	_____	_____	_____
10. iter, itineris	_____	_____	_____

Activity 22d Dative Forms of Adjectives

Give the dative forms of each of the following adjectives in the gender indicated by the nominative singular form:

	Dative Singular	Dative Plural
1. nocturnus	_____	_____
2. obēsa	_____	_____
3. fortis	_____	_____
4. sordidum	_____	_____
5. omne	_____	_____

Activity 22e Dative Forms of Pronouns

Give the dative forms of each of the following pronouns:

	Dative Singular	**Dative Plural**
1. vōs, *you*		_____
2. is, *he*	_____	
3. tū, *you*	_____	
4. ea, *she*	_____	
5. ego, *I*	_____	
6. id, *it* (neut.)	_____	
7. eī, *they* (masc.)		_____
8. nōs, *we*		_____
9. ea, *they* (neut.)		_____
10. eae, *they* (fem.)		_____

3rd Declension Adjectives of One Termination

Activity 22f *brevis* and *ingēns*

At the left, write the correct form of **brevis, -is, -e** *to modify each of the following nouns. At the right, write the correct form of* **ingēns, ingentis** *to modify each noun:*

Nominative

1. _____	virga	_____
2. _____	baculum	_____
3. _____	arbor	_____
4. _____	rāmus	_____
5. _____	corpus	_____

Accusative

6. _____	virgam	_____
7. _____	baculum	_____

8. _____ arborem   _____

9. _____ rāmum   _____

10. _____ corpus   _____

Ablative

11. _____ virgā   _____

12. _____ baculō   _____

13. _____ arbore   _____

14. _____ rāmō   _____

15. _____ corpore   _____

Building the Meaning

The Dative Case

Activity 22g Using the Dative Case

Give the Latin word or phrase that would translate the underlined English word or phrase:

1. At dawn Sextus shouted <u>to Marcus</u>, "At last we are going to Rome!" _____

2. Cornelius shouted <u>to the boys</u>, "It is necessary <u>for you</u> to climb into the carriage

   immediately." _____ _____

3. In the carriage Aurelia was scolding Cornelia, "It was not allowed <u>for you</u> to leave your

   bedroom." _____

4. The slaves prepared a very good dinner <u>for Cornelius and Marcus and Sextus</u>.

   _____

5. The soldier told <u>us</u> a story. _____

6. Sextus was asking many things when they approached <u>a huge building</u>.

   _____

Nouns: Dative or Ablative? How Do You Decide?

Activity 22h Deciding between the Dative and the Ablative Case

Read the following sentences carefully. Circle all words in the dative case and underline all words in the ablative case. If the ending of a word does not clearly identify its case, use the guidelines on page 191 of Book I on page 57 of Book IB to help you decide. Then translate the sentences:

1. Dum Cornēliī in caupōnā sē parābant, Eucleidēs mandāta servīs dabat.

_____

_____

2. Raedārius auxiliō servōrum caupōnis raedam ē fossā extrāxit.

_____

_____

3. Sextus cum raedāriō sedēbat et Mārcō clāmābat.

_____

4. Ūndecimā hōrā rūsticī bovēs tardōs baculīs et clāmōribus per viam incitābant.

_____

_____

5. Servī caupōnis cēnam viātōribus dēfessīs parāre possunt.

_____

_____

6. Interdiū nōn licet mercātōribus bona in urbem plaustrīs portāre.

_____

_____

7. Cornēlia cibum canibus bonīs dare volēbat.

_____

8. Necesse erat Mārcō lupum rāmō repellere.

_____

9. Postquam Aulus amīcō suō appāruit, Septimus somniō perterritus surrēxit.

_____

_____

10. Septimus, postquam stercus remōvit et corpus in plaustrō invēnit, omnia dē caupōne scelestō cīvibus explicāvit.

_____

_____

bona, -ōrum, n. pl., *goods, possessions*

Applying What You Have Learned

Activity 22i Writing the Language

Translate the following English sentences into Latin. Include all long marks. Use the stories and vocabulary lists in your textbook, as well as the vocabulary lists in this book, to help you:

1. Cornelius was showing huge buildings to the boys, while they were traveling to Rome.

_____

_____

2. Cornelius wanted to tell the children the story told about Caecilia Metella.

_____

_____

3. While they were approaching the Porta Capena, Titus was waiting for them near the gate.

_____

_____

4. Cornelius sent a letter and explained everything to Titus.

_____

5. It is necessary for the emperor to consult the senators immediately.

_____

Activity 22j Expanding Your English Vocabulary

Using the word bank below, write the word that could replace the italicized word or words in each sentence. Use the Latin words in parentheses to help determine the meaning of the English words. Then write the English translation of each Latin word in the word bank:

1. In his dealings with Aurelia, Cornelius did not want to seem *too submissive to his wife.*   _____

2. The emperor told the senators that he thought it was *compulsory* to provide free grain to the masses.   _____

3. The senator had to decide between constructing a free-standing tomb or a *small burial chamber cut into stone or native rock.*   _____

4. Aurelia saw no *advantage* in staying at the inn.   _____

5. Although it was scary at times, Marcus and Sextus would not *exchange* their adventure at the inn for any other experience.   _____

6. Some historians claim that the Roman Empire fell to the barbarians because the people had fallen into *luxuriously self-indulgent* habits.   _____

7. Aurelia had to admit that the innkeeper was a *kindly* man.   _____

8. The soldier's story was lengthy; it *took up* most of the night.   _____

9. Aurelia's room was in a terrible *condition.*   _____

10. The Cornelius family could not have predicted that their *helper* in distress would be an innkeeper.   _____

---

state (**stāre**) _____

benevolent (**bene**) _____ +

  (**volō**) _____

uxorious (**uxor**) _____

trade (**trādere**) _____

consumed (**sūmere**) _____

decadent (**dē**) _____ +

  (**cadere**) _____

mandatory (**mandātum**) _____

benefactor (**bene**) _____ +

  (**facere**) _____

sepulcher (**sepulcrum**) _____

benefit (**bene**) _____

Activity 22k Reading Latin

Look at the new vocabulary on the next page. Then read the story, noting occurrences and uses of the dative case. Reread the story for comprehension. Then answer the questions with complete Latin sentences:

Titus Gets Ready

In urbe Rōmā diēs iam calidus erat. Servī et ancillae Titī cibum coquēbant, domum pūrgābant, tacitē labōrābant quod dominum excitāre nōlēbant. Titus tamen in lectō iacēbat et stertēbat, immemor frātris Cornēliī.

Tandem servus Titī cubiculum intrāvit et dominum excitāvit. Titus invītus surrēxit et, "Fer ad mē cibum et tunicam pūram," servō clāmāvit. Brevī tempore servus tunicam et cibum ad dominum tulit. Dum auxiliō servī tunicam induit, Titus rogāvit, "Quota hōra est?"

"Est quīnta hōra, domine," respondit servus. "Nōndum est tempus cēnāre." Eō ipsō tempore alius servus Titī ad iānuam appāruit. "Est nūntius in ātriō, mī domine," inquit. "Epistulam tibi habet."

"Mehercule! Habetne mihi epistulam? Statim eum vocā," exclāmāvit Titus. Brevī tempore intrāvit nūntius, quī epistulam Titō trādidit. Titus epistulam lēgit. "Ēheu!" exclāmāvit Titus. "Necesse est mihi lectīcāriōs statim condūcere et frātrem et familiam eius ad Portam Capēnam excipere. Cūr mē nōn prius excitāvistī?"

"Frātrem et familiam iterum excipis? Nōnne heri ad urbem advēnērunt?" rogāvit servus.

"Minimē," respondit Titus. "Heri lectīcāriōs condūxī et ad Portam Capēnam iī. Multās hōrās ibi manēbam, sed frāter meus numquam advēnit. Tandem domum rediī. Haec epistula rem explicat. Cornēlius aliquid malī accēpit et familia in caupōnā pernoctāvit. Nunc omnēs iterum in itinere sunt; Cornēlius ad Portam Capēnam sextā hōrā advenīre vult. Ī statim ad Forum! Celeriter meō frātrī Cornēliō et Aurēliae et Cornēliae condūc lectīcāriōs! Aliī lectīcāriī mē ad Portam Capēnam ferent."

Celeriter servī omnia Titō parāvērunt. "Quam dēfessus sum!" exclāmāvit Titus.

> **domum,** *house,* *home*
>
> **stertō, stertere, stertuī,** *to snore*
>
> **pūrus, -a, -um,** *clean*
>
> **ātrium, -ī,** n., *atrium,* *main room*
>
> **lectīcārius, -ī,** m., *litter-bearer*
>
> **condūcō, condūcere, condūxī, conductus,** *to hire*
>
> **familia, -ae,** f., *family,* *household*
>
> **eius,** *his*
>
> **prius,** adv., *earlier*
>
> **aliquid malī,** *something bad*
>
> **accipiō, accipere, accēpī, acceptus,** *to receive*
>
> **ferent,** *will carry*

1. Cui surgere māne nōn necesse fuit?

_____

2. Cui Titus clāmāvit?

_____

3. Cui nūntius epistulam trādidit?

_____

4. Quibus Titus lectīcāriōs condūcere voluit?

_____

5. Quibus Titus exclāmāvit "Quam dēfessus sum!"?

_____

AT THE PORTA CAPENA

In addition to vocabulary and the story, the activities in this chapter focus on:
1. the use of adjectives as substantives.
2. the future tense of regular verbs.
3. determining whether verbs with identical endings are in the present or future tense.
4. the future tense of irregular verbs.

Vocabulary

Activity 23a Vocabulary

Study the vocabulary list on pages 246–247 alone or with a partner.

The Story

Activity 23b Vocabulary in Context

Fill in the blanks with Latin words to match the English cues:

1. Cīvēs _____ _____ currēbant. (this way and that)

2. Līberī _____ ubi _____ hominum vīdērunt.
   (were amazed) (crowd)

3. _____ erant clāmōrēs mercātōrum. (On all sides)

4. Titus līberōs _____ _____ _____
   salūtāvit. (with very great joy)

5. Ubi _____ advēnērunt, Cornēliī ē raedā _____. (there)
   (got down from)

6. Ego puerōs _____ et omnia _____ eīs explicābō.
   (will take care of) (the wonderful things)

7. Ūndecimā hōrā ego puerōs domum _____. (will take)

8. In _____, quās Titus condūxit, domum mox ībimus. (the litters)

9. Cornēlius lectīcāriōs iussit sē et Aurēliam et Cornēliam _____
   _____ ferre. (home) (first)

10. Lectīcāriī eōs domum _____. (will carry)

11. Dum domum eunt, Syrus raedārius raedam ab urbe _____. (will drive)

12. Ubi Cornēlius domum _____, sē lāvit et aliam togam praetextam

_____. (arrived) (put on)

13. Crās fortasse omnēs līberī Cūriam et Forum _____. (will see)

Building the Meaning

Adjectives as Substantives

Activity 23c Adjectives as Substantives

Fill in the blanks with adjectives used as substantives to match the English cues:

1. _____ ad Portam Capēnam advenient. (many men)

2. _____ ē raedīs dēscendunt. (many women)

3. Cornēliī _____ in Viā Appiā cōnspexērunt. (many men)

4. Cornēliī _____ in Viā Appiā nōn cōnspexērunt. (many women)

5. _____ hūc illūc currēbant. (Everyone)

6. Viātōrēs _____ vidēbunt. (many things)

Forms

Verbs: Future Tense I

Activity 23d Changing Regular Verbs to the Future Tense

Identify the conjugation of each verb, and then change it to the future tense, keeping the same person and number:

1. dēscendunt _____ _____

2. exspectat _____ _____

3. pluit _____ _____

4. nārrāmus _____ _____

5. excipiunt _____ _____

6. videō _____ _____

7. condūcō _____ _____

8. dormītis _____ _____

9. cōnstituit _____ _____

10. sedētis _____ _____

Activity 23e The Future Tense of Regular Verbs in Sentences

Underline the words that serve as subjects in the following sentences. Then fill in the correct future tense form of the verbs in parentheses to complete the sentences:

1. Ego, sī hīc _____, certē dīligenter _____. (manēre)
   (labōrāre)

2. Ego in lectīcā _____ et lectīcāriī mē domum _____.
   (cōnsīdere) (portāre)

3. Tū togam praetextam _____. (induere)

4. Titus, sī ad Portam Capēnam _____, Cornēliōs ibi

   _____. (manēre) (excipere)

5. Ubi ego vōs per urbem _____, vōs multa et mīra _____.
   (dūcere) (vidēre)

Building the Meaning

Present or Future Tense? How Do You Decide?

Activity 23f Look-Alikes: Identifying Verbs as Present or Future

Identify the conjugation of each verb, and then circle the future tense verb in each pair:

1. manēs _____ sūmēs _____

2. movēmus _____ agēmus _____

3. dīcent _____ tacent _____

4. accidet _____ licet _____

5. iubētis _____ cadētis _____

6. current _____ rīdent _____

7. eram _____ cōnstituam _____

8. reprehendent _____ respondent _____

9. pōnō _____ erō _____

10. pōnēmus _____ timēmus _____

Verbs: Future Tense II

Activity 23g Changing Irregular Verbs to the Future Tense

Change the following verbs to the future tense, keeping the same person and number:

1. vīs _____

2. est _____

3. possumus _____

4. eunt _____

5. fers _____

6. sunt _____

7. nōlumus _____

8. potestis _____

9. ferunt _____

10. nōn vult _____

11. redeō _____

12. absumus _____

13. vultis _____

14. ferō _____

15. potes _____

Activity 23h The Future Tense of Irregular Verbs in Sentences

Underline the words that serve as subjects in the following sentences. Then fill in the correct future tense form of the verbs in parentheses to complete the sentences:

1. Servī cistās in cubiculum _____. (ferre)

2. Quō tū crās _____, Tite? Nōnne tū in urbem _____? (īre) (exīre)

3. Nōs patrī rem explicāre nōn _____. (posse)

4. Senātor ad Cūriam crās _____. (īre)

5. Aurēlia et Cornēlia domum redīre _____. (velle)

6. Nōnne tū Circum Maximum vīsitāre _____? (velle)

7. Sī dominus _____, servī scelestī strēnuē labōrāre _____.
(abesse) (nōlle)

8. Aurēlia et Cornēlia domum lectīcīs _____. (redīre)

9. Ecce, domina! Ego et aliī servī tē domum in lectīcā _____. (ferre)

10. Crās tū et Cornēlia in urbem cum patre _____. (exīre)

Applying What You Have Learned

Activity 23i Writing the Language

*Translate the following English sentences into Latin. Include all long marks. Use the stories
and vocabulary lists in your textbook, as well as the vocabulary lists in this book, to help you:*

1. Titus, while he was walking to the Porta Capena, saw a good friend and greeted (him).

_____

_____

2. "Hello, Lucius," said Titus, "it is necessary for me to hurry because today my brother will
arrive with his wife and children."

_____

_____

3. "First, however, I will hire litter-bearers because it will be necessary for Cornelius to go to the Senate House immediately."

_____

_____

4. "There is always a big crowd near the Porta Capena," replied Lucius. "You will be amazed."

_____

_____

5. "Will you go to the Senate House with Cornelius?" asked Lucius.

_____

_____

6. "No," replied Titus, "I will lead the boys home. They will see many wonderful things."

_____

_____

Lucius, **Lūcius, -ī,** m.

Activity 23j Expanding Your English Vocabulary

For each italicized English word below, give the related Latin word and below it the meaning of that Latin word. Then complete each sentence by filling in a word at the right:

Latin Word
Meaning of the Latin Word

If you …

1. _____   have an *agile* mind, you have
a mind that is   _____

_____

2. _____   create an *agenda*, you make a
list of things to be   _____

_____

3. _____   are doing *domestic* chores,
you are doing work at   _____

_____

4. _____
have seen a *miraculous* event,
you have seen an event that is
_____

_____

5. _____
are *stupefied* by what you see, you
are totally _____ by it.
_____

_____

6. _____
attend *primary* school, you are in the
_____ stages of your schooling.
_____

_____

7. _____
play in an *intramural* competition,
you play against students who
study within the _____ of
_____
your own school.

8. _____
consider the *facts*, you consider
only those things that were
_____

_____

9. _____
have *satisfied* your appetite,
you have eaten
_____

_____

10. _____
acquiesce in a decision, you raise
no objection, but instead you keep
_____

_____

Activity 23k Reading Latin

Look at the new vocabulary following this story. Then read the story, noting the tenses of verbs carefully. Reread the Latin for comprehension. Then mark whether each statement about the story is V = Vērum (True) or F = Falsum (False):

"I Too Want to See the City!"

Extrā urbem Cornēlia laeta ē raedā dēscendit et patruum Titum cum gaudiō salūtāvit. Dum Titus rem quandam Cornēliō explicābat, spectābat Cornēlia multōs quī hūc illūc festīnābant. Suprā capita erant Aqua Mārcia et mūrus urbis.

"Venī nōbīscum, Cornēlia," inquit Aurēlia. "Raedam hīc relinquēmus et in lectīcīs sedēbimus. Lectīcāriī nōs domum ferent. Pater tuus alterā lectīcā domum petet. Eō celeriter adveniēmus."

"Quid dē puerīs?" rogāvit puella. "Cūr cum Titō et Eucleide adhūc stant?"

"Puerī cum patruō tuō hīc manēbunt. Titus eōs per urbem dūcet et multa eīs in itinere mōnstrābit. Puerī domum nunc īre nōlunt. Pater domum celerrimē īre vult, nam brevī tempore ad Cūriam ībit. Necesse est nōbīs cum patre statim īre."

Invīta in lectīcam ascendit Cornēlia. "Ego quoque," inquit, "multa in itinere vidēre volō." "Cōnspiciēmus mīra, quae tibi explicābō," inquit Aurēlia. "In urbe sunt multa nova quae vidēre poterimus." Tum lectīcāriī lectīcam in umerōs sustulērunt. Mox lectīcāriī per viās urbis Cornēliōs ferēbant. Aurēlia, "Cum domum adveniēmus," inquit, "omnēs et omnia īnspicere volam."

Fēminae ingentēs īnsulās in itinere vīdērunt in quibus pauperēs habitābant. Etiam cōnspexērunt mercātōrēs quī in tabernīs erant, praeclārōs quōs servī in lectīcīs ferēbant, servōs et cīvēs quī in viīs ambulābant. Tandem domum magnam et amoenam cōnspexērunt. "Eugepae!" clāmāvit Cornēlia. "Nostram domum videō! Laeta sum domī esse."

rem quandam, *a certain matter*
caput, capitis, n., *head*
umerus, -ī, m. *shoulder*
tollō, tollere, sustulī, sublātus, *to lift*, *raise*, *raise up*

īnsula, -ae, f., *apartment building*
pauper, pauperis, m., *poor person*
taberna, -ae, f., *shop*
amoenus, -a, -um, *pleasant*
domī, *at home*

1. Puerī in lectīcīs domum ībunt.   V   F
2. Cornēlia in lectīcam ascendet.   V   F
3. Aurēlia Cornēliae mīra et nova in itinere explicābit.   V   F
4. Cornēlius omnēs et omnia domī īnspiciet.   V   F
5. Fēminae praeclārōs quōs servī in lectīcīs ferēbant vīdērunt.   V   F

ALWAYS TOMORROW

> *In addition to vocabulary and the story, the activities in this chapter focus on:*
> 1. the dative case used with intransitive compound verbs.
> 2. the ablative case without a preposition to show cause.
> 3. the pluperfect tense of verbs.
> 4. the future perfect tense of verbs.

Vocabulary

Activity 24a Vocabulary

Study the vocabulary list on page 248 alone or with a partner.

The Story

Activity 24b Dictation and Vocabulary

Fill in the blanks as your teacher reads the story aloud. Then go back and write the meanings of the Latin words in the spaces provided. As you do so, add pronouns as subjects for any verbs that do not have expressed subjects in the Latin:

Simulac Titus et puerī et Eucleidēs urbem per Portam Capēnam **1.** _____

= _____, clāmāvit Sextus, "Quid nōs prīmum faciēmus? Quō

2. _____ = _____? Vīsitābimusne—?"

"Quō tū nōs dūcēs, patrue?" interpellāvit Mārcus. "Vidēbimusne Cūriam et Forum? Sextus

multa dē Rōmā **3.** _____ = _____ et audīvit et nunc, patrue,

omnia vidēre vult."

Titus, "Tacēte! Tacēte!" inquit. "Forum crās **4.** _____ =

_____. Crās, Eucleidēs, tibi **5.** _____ =

_____ puerōs eō dūcere. Tum erit satis temporis. Hodiē tamen, puerī, vōs

domum per urbem dūcam et omnia in itinere vōbīs dēmōnstrābō."

Iam **6.** _____ = _____ ad Circum Maximum, quī nōn

procul aberat. Stupuit Sextus ubi **7.** _____ = _____ Circī

Maximī vīdit. Mārcus quoque stupuit, quamquam Circum anteā **8.** _____ =

_____. Stupuit Titus, **9.** _____ = _____

nōn mōle, sed silentiō Circī.

"Ēheu! Ēheu!" inquit Titus. "Hodiē Circus est **10.** _____ =

_____. Tribus diēbus tamen prīnceps ipse, Titus Flāvius Vespasiānus,

11. _____ = _____ magnificōs faciet."

"Nōnne tū nōs eō **12.** _____ = _____ rogāvit Mārcus.

"Ēheu! Ego nōn poterō vōs dūcere," inquit Titus. "**13.** _____ =

_____ Eucleidēs vōs dūcet."

"Minimē!" respondit Sextus. "**14.** _____ = _____, nōn

lūdōs amat Eucleidēs."

"Agite, puerī!" interpellāvit Titus. "Nunc **15.** _____ =

_____ Montem Palātīnum et Forum intrābimus ad **16.** _____

= _____ Tiberiī. Ibi fortasse patrī tuō occurrēmus, Mārce. Mox senātōrēs ē

Cūriā exībunt."

Itaque Circum **17.** _____ = _____ et Palātīnum

circumiērunt. Titus in itinere mōnstrāvit puerīs mīra aedificia quae prīncipēs in Palātīnō

18. _____ = _____.

Tandem ad arcum Tiberiī advēnērunt, iam labōre et **19.** _____ =

_____ dēfessī. "Hic est arcus," inquit Titus, "quem—" "Omnia vidēre

20. _____ = _____ crās," interpellāvit Cornēlius, quī eō ipsō

tempore ad arcum ē Cūriā advēnerat. "Cum ad Forum crās **21.** _____ =

_____, Eucleidēs omnia vōbīs explicābit. Iam sērō est. Agite! Iam domum

22. _____ = _____."

Building the Meaning

Dative with Intransitive Compound Verbs

Activity 24c Dative with Intransitive Compound Verbs

Circle the intransitive compound verbs in the following sentences. Then fill in the correct dative ending to complete the form of each noun. Be sure to check the declension of each noun, and use singular or plural forms as specified for each sentence:

1. Dum Cornēliī urb_____ appropinquābant, multa sepulcra vidēbant. (sing.)

2. Clāmōrem et frāgōrem audīvērunt quod Port_____ Capēn _____ appropinquābant. (sing.)

3. Cornēlius frātr_____ occurrit et laetus eum salūtāvit. (sing.)

4. Lectīcāriī lectīcās portābant et Cornēli_____ occurrērunt. (pl.)

5. Cornēlius ad Cūriam ībit quod prīncip_____ occurrere vult. (sing.)

Ablative of Cause

Activity 24d Ablative of Cause

Combine the following sentences by blending an element of the second into the first, using an ablative of cause. The first is done for you:

1. Sextus perterritus nōn obdormīvit. Fābulam audīvit.

   Sextus fābulā perterritus nōn obdormīvit. _____.

2. Raeda est in fossā. Tua est culpa.

   _____

3. Magna īra Dāvum commōvit. Servum verberat.

   _____

4. Iter erat longum. Aurēlia dēfessa sē quiētī dedit.

   _____

5. Sextus canēs magnōs videt. Sextus perterritus fugit.

   _____

6. Rūsticī multōs labōrēs cōnfēcerant. Rūsticī dēfessī sub arboribus quiēscēbant.

_____

7. Parentēs clāmōrēs audīvērunt. Parentēs sollicitī līberōs petēbant.

_____

Forms

Verbs: Pluperfect Tense

Activity 24e Forming the Pluperfect Tense

Write the perfect stem of the following verbs in the blank next to each form. Then change each verb to the pluperfect tense, keeping the same person and number:

	Perfect Stem	**Pluperfect Form**
1. appārent	_____	_____
2. removēmus	_____	_____
3. adiuvās	_____	_____
4. dat	_____	_____
5. sūmitis	_____	_____
6. īs	_____	_____
7. ferunt	_____	_____
8. agimus	_____	_____
9. cōnspiciō	_____	_____
10. iubēs	_____	_____
11. pōnitis	_____	_____
12. sum	_____	_____

Verbs: Future Perfect Tense

Activity 24f Forming the Future Perfect Tense

Write the perfect stem of the following verbs in the blank next to each form. Then change each verb to the future perfect tense, keeping the same person and number:

	Perfect Stem	Future Perfect Form
1. aedificāmus	_____	_____
2. occurritis	_____	_____
3. vult	_____	_____
4. stupēs	_____	_____
5. fīnit	_____	_____
6. possumus	_____	_____
7. colit	_____	_____
8. nōlō	_____	_____
9. cōgitant	_____	_____
10. ferunt	_____	_____
11. cōnspicimus	_____	_____
12. induis	_____	_____
13. īmus	_____	_____
14. conicit	_____	_____

Activity 24g Pluperfect and Future Perfect

Underline all words that serve as subjects in the following sentences. Then fill in the blanks with the correct forms of the Latin verbs to match the English cues. Make sure to note the tense of the verb carefully:

1. Iam puerī urbem _____. (had entered)

2. Puerī, sī Circum Maximum _____, laetī domum ībunt.
   (will have seen/see)

3. Sī puerī Cornēliō in Forō _____, eōs domum dūcet. (will have met/meet)

4. Sextus, quī numquam anteā Rōmae _____, attonitus erat. (had been)

5. Stupuit Sextus ubi Circum vīdit quod numquam anteā tāle aedificium

_____. (had seen)

6. Sī sērō domum _____, pater īrātus erit. (we will have arrived/we arrive)

7. Cum in urbem crās _____, Sexte, Circum Maximum iterum vidēbis.
   (you will have descended/you descend)

8. Nisi prīmā lūce _____, puerī, vōs in urbem nōn dūcam. (you will have
   gotten up/you get up)

9. Puerī cubitum īre timēbant quod fābulam dē Aulī morte nārrātam _____.
   (they had heard)

10. Ille caupō, sī Aulus in caupōnam _____, eum certē necābit. (will have
    entered/enters)

Applying What You Have Learned

Activity 24h Writing the Language

*Translate the following English sentences into Latin. Include all long marks. Use the stories
and vocabulary lists in your textbook, as well as the vocabulary lists in this book, to help you:*

1. The boys, who had left the Circus Maximus and gone around the Palatine Hill, descended to
   the Forum.

   _____

   _____

2. They were tired from the labor and heat.

   _____

3. Near the Arch of Tiberius they met Cornelius.

   _____

4. Cornelius had already taken the boys home. "Tomorrow," said Cornelius, "you will see all the
   wonderful buildings in the city."

   _____

   _____

5. "In three days, when you (*pl.*) and Eucleides will have entered/enter the Circus Maximus, you will see the games."

_____

_____

Activity 24i Expanding Your English Vocabulary

Using the word bank below, write the word that could replace the italicized word or words in each sentence. Use the Latin words in parentheses to help determine the meaning of the English words. Then write the English translation of each Latin word in the word bank:

1. Eucleides had an extensive *collection of books*. _____

2. Marcus thought that Sextus's story of the cat and mouse was *silly*. _____

3. Wheeled vehicles had no *permission* to enter the city until nightfall. _____

4. On the Palatine Hill stood the *grand residence* of the emperor. _____

5. Sextus was amazed by the noise and *movement* of the crowd. _____

6. Titus pointed to the words *written* on the arch. _____

7. The boys struggled to make out the inscription that was *unreadable* in the glare of the sun. _____

8. The night spent in the inn was marked by many strange *happenings*. _____

9. Through the mist, they could see the colorful *curve* of a rainbow. _____

10. Eucleides will *show* the proper way to write the Greek alphabet. _____

arc (**arcus**) _____	demonstrate (**dēmōnstrāre**) _____
illegible (**legere**) _____	_____
inscribed (**in**) _____ +	license (**licēre**) _____
(**scrībere**) _____	library (**liber**) _____
ludicrous (**lūdī**) _____	occurrences (**occurrere**) _____
motion (**movēre**) _____	palace (**Palātīnus**) _____

Activity 24j Reading Latin

Look at the new vocabulary beneath this story. Then read the story, noting the tenses of verbs carefully. Reread the Latin for comprehension. Then rewrite the sentences on the next page so that the statements about the story are true:

Home at Last

Ubi lectīcāriī ad iānuam advēnērunt, servī et ancillae omnia dominō et dominae iam parāverant. Cornēliī ad iānuam occurrērunt iānitōrī, quī dominum et dominam et Cornēliam salūtāvit. Iānitor, "Quam laetī," inquit, "servī vestrī vōs omnēs excipient!" Cornēlius, quī ē lectīcā dēscenderat et iānitōrem salūtāverat, cum uxōre et fīliā domum intrāvit. Alius servus, nōmine Tīrō, eōs maximō cum gaudiō excēpit.

Tīrō, "Statim tē lavāre poteris, domine," inquit, "quod servī omnia tibi parāvērunt." Cornēlius ad cubiculum iam festīnāverat, et Tīrō ad fēminās sē vertit.

Aurēlia Tīrōnī, "Simulac servī cistās nostrās ad cubicula tulerint," inquit, "ego et Cornēlia nōs quiētī dabimus. Prīmum tamen necesse est mihi domum īnspicere. Certē servīs et ancillīs cōnfīdō, sed ego ipsa omnia vidēre volō. Per tōtam domum mē dūc, Tīrō. Venī mēcum, Cornēlia."

Dum māter et fīlia culīnae cum Tīrōne appropinquābant, servī et ancillae capita dēmittēbant quod dominam timēbant. Aurēlia, ubi tōtam domum īnspexerat, "Sī lectōs et cubicula nōbīs parāveritis, nōs quiētī statim dabimus," inquit. "Ego et Cornēlia itinere dēfessae sumus."

sē, *himself*
cōnfīdō, cōnfīdere + dat., *to give trust (to), trust*
caput, capitis, n., *head*
dēmittō, dēmittere, dēmīsī, dēmissus, *to lower*
    caput dēmittere, *to bow the head*

1. Iānitor excēpit dominum et dominam et fīliam, ubi domum circumierant.

   _____

2. Simulac Cornēliī exiērunt, Tīrō eōs salūtāvit.

   _____

3. Quod servī omnēs eōs salūtāvērunt, Cornēlius sē lavāre poterit.

   _____

4. Simulac Aurēlia omnia relīquerit, sē quiētī dabit.

   _____

5. Aurēlia, quod servōs et ancillās timēbat, omnia vidēre voluit.

   _____

6. Cum servī et ancillae lectōs et cistās cēlāverint, Aurēlia et Cornēlia sē quiētī dabunt.

   _____

FIRST MORNING IN ROME

> *In addition to vocabulary and the story, the activities in this chapter focus on:*
> 1. 4th and 5th declension nouns.
> 2. the genitive case in partitive constructions.

Vocabulary

Activity 25a Vocabulary

Study the vocabulary list on pages 249–250 alone or with a partner.

The Story

Activity 25b Dictation and Vocabulary

Fill in the blanks as your teacher reads the story aloud. Then go back and write the meanings of the Latin words in the spaces provided. As you do so, add pronouns as subjects for any verbs that do not have expressed subjects in the Latin:

Iam diēs erat. Magnus erat **1.** _____ = _____ in

urbe. Servī ad Forum magnō **2.** _____ = _____ onera

ferēbant. Undique clāmor et strepitus! Sed nihil clāmōris, nihil **3.** _____ =

_____ ad Mārcum pervēnit. In lectō stertēbat, nam dēfessus erat. Sextus

quoque in lectō manēbat sed **4.** _____ = _____ nōn poterat.

Clāmōribus et strepitū **5.** _____ = _____, iam cōgitābat dē

omnibus **6.** _____ = _____ quās Titus heri nārrāverat. "Quid

hodiē vidēbimus? Cornēliusne nōs in Forum dūcet? Ego certē Forum et Cūriam et senātōrēs

vidēre volō."

Intereā Eucleidēs, quī prīmā lūce exierat, iam domum **7.** _____ =

_____. Statim cubiculum puerōrum petīvit et, "Eho, puerī!" inquit. "Cūr

nōndum surrēxistis? **8.** _____ = _____ duās hōrās ego

surrēxī. Quod novum librum emere volēbam, in Argīlētum māne dēscendī ad

9. _____ = _____ quandam ubi in

10. _____ = _____ nōmina multōrum

11. _____ = _____ vidēre potes. Catullus, Flaccus—"

At puerī celeriter interpellāvērunt quod Eucleidēs, ut 12. _____ = _____ sciēbant, semper 13. _____ = _____ novī docēre volēbat. "Quid in viīs vīdistī?"

Eucleidēs, "Nihil," inquit, "nisi miserum hominem 14. _____ = _____ oppressum. Bovēs lapidēs 15. _____ = _____ in plaustrō trahēbant ad novum aedificium quod Caesar prope Domum Auream cōnficit. Illud aedificium est ingēns 16. _____ = _____ et mox prīnceps lūdōs ibi faciet. Sī bonī puerī 17. _____ = _____, fortasse ad lūdōs ībitis."

Forms

Nouns: 4th and 5th Declensions

Activity 25c Using 4th Declension Nouns

Fill in the blanks with the proper forms of the noun **strepitus, -ūs,** *m. Determine the function of the noun in each sentence before you add a case ending:*

1. Sextus magnum _____ in viā audīvit.

2. Nihil _____ in viā erat. (sing.)

3. Plaustra magnō cum _____ nocte per viās onera ferēbant.

4. Mārcus dormiēbat et stertēbat. Magnōs _____ plaustrōrum in viā nōn audīvit.

5. Tandem Mārcus multīs clāmōribus et magnīs _____ excitātus ē lectō surrēxit.

6. Ingēns _____ aurīgārum puerōs dormientēs excitāvit.

7. _____ multōrum vehiculōrum nocte in viīs Rōmae erat.

Activity 25d Using 5th Declension Nouns

Fill in the blanks with the proper forms of the noun **rēs, reī,** *f. Determine the function*
of the noun in each sentence before you add a case ending:

1. Sextus Mārcō _____ tōtam explicāvit.

2. Quās _____ hodiē vidēre vultis?

3. Servī multīs _____ plaustra onerābant.

4. Plaustrum erat plēnum multārum _____.

5. Multae _____ nōs in urbe nocte vexābant.

6. Pecūnia est _____ omnium optima.

7. Quae est causa huius _____ malae?

8. Eucleidēs librum dē _____ rūsticā legit.

    onerō, -āre, -āvī, -ātus, *to load*

Building the Meaning

The Partitive Genitive or Genitive of the Whole

Activity 25e Partitive Genitive

Translate the following Latin phrases that use the partitive genitive:

1. satis temporis   _____

2. nihil temporis   _____

3. multum temporis   _____

4. satis pecūniae   _____

5. nihil pecūniae   _____

6. multum pecūniae   _____

7. multum strepitūs   _____

8. multum clāmōris   _____

9. multum tumultūs   _____

10. aliquid novī   _____

Applying What You Have Learned

Activity 25f Writing the Language

Translate the following English sentences into Latin. Include all long marks. Use the stories and vocabulary lists in your textbook, as well as the vocabulary lists in this book, to help you:

1. There is always much commotion on the streets of Rome.

   _____

2. During the day there is much noise, much shouting in the streets of the city.

   _____

   _____

3. The emperor is always building something new; therefore slaves drag stones toward the Forum.

   _____

   _____

4. There is not enough time to see everything and do everything.

   _____

5. While we are living in the city, we never have enough money.

   _____

Activity 25g Expanding Your English Vocabulary

For each italicized English word, give the related Latin word and below it the meaning of that Latin word. Then complete each sentence by filling in a word at the right:

Latin Word
Meaning of the Latin Word

If you ...

1. _____   hear a *tumult* in the city
                              streets, you hear

   _____   _____

2. _____   visit a *tavern* today, you do
                              not find a _____, as the Latin   _____
   _____   source word suggests, but
                              instead a saloon or a bar.

3. _____   are operating a *tractor*,
                              you are operating a vehicle
   _____   designed to   _____

4. _____   are a *vintner*, you are a
                              merchant who sells
   _____   _____

5. _____   are a people being *oppressed*
                              by a tyrannical leader, you can
   _____   feel as if you are being   _____

6. _____   work as a *lapidary*, you cut,
                              polish, and engrave precious
   _____   _____

7. _____   have *stertorous* breathing, you
                              make _____ sounds.
   _____   _____

8. _____   lose *traction* in a tug-of-war,
                              you are unable to _____ on
   _____   the rope.   _____

9. _____   are in the *capital* of a country
                              you are in the city where the
   _____   _____ of state resides.   _____

10. _____   attend a *tumultuous* meeting,
                              you attend a meeting that is   _____
   _____

Activity 25h Reading Latin

Look at the new vocabulary on the next page. Then read the story, noting the forms of 4th and 5th declension nouns and partitive genitives. Reread the Latin for comprehension. Then match the first part of each sentence that follows to the phrase or clause that correctly completes it:

Out on the Town

Diēs erat et Mārcus et Sextus adhūc in lectīs stertēbant cum intrāvit Eucleidēs, quī exclāmāvit, "Tempus est surgere, puerī. Tempus est nōbīs urbem Sextō mōnstrāre et Forum et Cūriam et multōs arcūs et aquaeductūs vidēre. Cum tunicās et togās indueritis, in urbem exībimus." Laetī erant puerī, nam in urbe erant multa quae nōndum vīderant.

Puerī, ubi surrēxērunt et vestēs induērunt, in ātriō domūs Eucleidī occurrērunt. Eucleidēs et puerī exiērunt et per magnam urbem multās hōrās ambulābant. Illā nocte, ubi Mārcus et Sextus domum rediērunt, Cornēlia frātrem et Sextum multa rogāvit.

Cornēlia: Quid in urbe fēcistī, Mārce?

Mārcus: Multa et mīra Sextō dēmōnstrāvī. Simulac in viam exiimus, multōs sonitūs audīvimus. Magnus erat tumultus. Audīvimus tumultum turbae et rīsūs cīvium quī praeterībant.

Cornēlia: Vīdistīne aliquid novī, Sexte?

Sextus: Numquam anteā tantum numerum hominum vīderam. Etiam domūs praeclārōrum virōrum et mercātōrēs et tabernās et aedificia Forī vīdimus. Quam ingēns est Rōma! Parvam modo partem urbis vīdimus! Satis temporis omnia vidēre nōn habuimus.

Mārcus: Omnēs novem Virginēs Vestālēs in Forō Rōmānō vīdimus. Ad
Ātrium Vestae, quod est domus eārum, redībant. Virginēs Vestāles
ignem sacrum in aede Vestae cūrant. Īnfulās et vittās gerēbant.

Cornēlia: Dēlectāvēruntne tē Vestālēs, Sexte?

Sextus: Fortasse mē paulum dēlectāvērunt, sed gladiātōrēs et aurīgas
vidēre valdē volō!

ātrium, -ī, n., *atrium, main room*

parvus, -a, -um, *small*

Vesta, -ae, f., *Vesta (goddess of the hearth)*

eārum, *their* (fem. pl.)

sacer, sacra, sacrum, *holy, sacred*

aedēs, aedis, f., *temple*

īnfula, -ae, f., *woolen headband (a special long headdress worn by priests and
priestesses)*

vitta, -ae, f., *woolen ribbon (knotted onto an **īnfula**)*

dēlectō, -āre, -āvī, -ātus, *to delight, amuse, please*

paulum, adv., *a little, somewhat*

1. Eucleidēs puerōs excitāvit _____

2. Puerī cum Eucleide per urbem multās
hōrās ambulābant et _____

3. Puerī et Eucleidēs domum pervēnērunt
_____

4. Sextus multa et mīra vīdit _____

5. Puerī parvam modo partem urbis
vīdērunt _____

6. Vidēre Virginēs Vestālēs prope Ātrium
Vestae _____

a. quod Rōma est urbs ingēns.

b. postquam per urbem multās hōrās
ambulāvērunt.

c. Sextum paulum dēlectāvit.

d. quod Sextō multa in urbe
mōnstrāre voluit.

e. quae Mārcus eī dēmōnstrāvit.

f. domūs praeclārōrum virōrum et mercātōrēs
et tabernās et aedificia Forī vīdērunt.

A Grim Lesson

In addition to vocabulary and the story, the activities in this chapter focus on:
1. forms of the demonstrative adjectives and pronouns **hic** and **ille**.
2. **hic** and **ille** in sentences.

Vocabulary

Activity 26a Vocabulary

Study the vocabulary list on pages 251–252 alone or with a partner.

The Story

Activity 26b Who Said That?

Without looking in your textbook, match the quotations below with the characters who said them in the story in Chapter 26. Write C for **Cornēlius**, M for **Mārcus**, P for **praedōnēs**, and S for **Sextus**:

1. _____ Nunc necesse est vōbīs cubitum īre.

2. _____ Quō abīs, parvule?

3. _____ Nōs in urbem exīre volumus sōlī. Cūr nōn licet?

4. _____ Cavē illōs hominēs!

5. _____ Heri nūllōs hominēs scelestōs in urbe vīdī.

6. _____ Nēmō nunc poterit tē servāre.

7. _____ Est perīculōsum sine custōde exīre in viās huius urbis.

8. _____ Fer auxilium! Fer auxilium!

9. _____ Nihil pecūniae habeō.

10. _____ Quid hodiē vīdistis, puerī?

11. _____ Interdiū certē praedōnēs nōbīs nōn nocēbunt.

12. _____ Tū es captīvus noster neque ad patrem redībis.

13. _____ Quandō Circum Maximum vīsitābimus?

Forms

Demonstrative Adjectives and Pronouns: *hic* and *ille*

Activity 26c Writing Adjectives to Agree with Nouns

*In the left-hand column, write the correct form of **hic, haec, hoc** to go with each noun; in the right-hand column write the correct form of **ille, illa, illud** to go with each noun. First determine the declension, gender, case, and number of the nouns, then write forms of **hic** and **ille** that agree with the nouns. The nouns used are in the word bank.*

hic, haec, hoc   **ille, illa, illud**

1. _____ aedificium   16. _____ cēnae (nom.)

2. _____ praedōnem   17. _____ praedōnēs (acc.)

3. _____ rēs (acc.)   18. _____ urbs

4. _____ arcū   19. _____ oculum

5. _____ oculī (nom.)   20. _____ urbis

6. _____ urbium   21. _____ aedificiīs

7. _____ cēnae (gen.)   22. _____ nōmine

8. _____ praedō   23. _____ oculōs

9. _____ nōmen   24. _____ praedōnibus

10. _____ rē   25. _____ rērum

11. _____ urbī   26. _____ cēnam

12. _____ aedificiī   27. _____ praedōnēs (nom.)

13. _____ arcuum   28. _____ oculōrum

14. _____ oculō (abl.)   29. _____ arcuī

15. _____ aedificia   30. _____ oculus

aedificium, -ī, n.	**oculus, -ī,** m.
arcus, -ūs, m.	**praedō, praedōnis,** m.
cēna, -ae, f.	**rēs, reī,** f.
nōmen, nōminis, n.	**urbs, urbis,** f.

Activity 26d Using *hic* and *ille* in Sentences

*Determine which noun is to be modified and identify its declension, gender, case, and number. Then fill in each blank with the proper form of **hic** or **ille** to agree with the noun in gender, case, and number.*

1. "Cavē _____ praedōnēs!" clāmāvit ūnus ex _____ cīvibus. (those) (these)

2. Pater _____ puerī est _____ senātor. (this) (that)

3. Cīvēs pecūniam in _____ viā _____ mercātōrī dabant. (this) (that)

4. _____ praedōnēs certē _____ bona arripient. (These) (those)

5. Eucleidēs _____ rem _____ puerīs explicābat. (this) (those)

6. In postibus _____ tabernārum _____ nōmina invēnimus. (those) (these)

7. Puerī in _____ partem urbis sine _____ custōde nōn dēscendent. (that) (this)

8. _____ diē caupō scelestus _____ hospitem necāvit. (That) (this)

9. Aurēlia neque _____ caupōnam neque _____ caupōnem amat. (that) (that)

10. Ego _____ gladium _____ manū strīnxī. (this) (this)

Applying What You Have Learned

Activity 26e Writing the Language

Translate the following English sentences into Latin. Include all long marks. Use the stories and vocabulary lists in your textbook, as well as the vocabulary lists in this book, to help you:

1. It is dangerous to walk through the streets of this city without a guard. Surely you know this, Marcus, don't you?

   _____

   _____

2. While they were saying these things, those wicked robbers drew (their) swords.

_____

3. Beware, wicked ones! The father of this boy is a distinguished senator.

_____

4. These boys were afraid to meet those wicked men again.

_____

5. That dream frightened me very much.

_____

Activity 26f **Expanding Your English Vocabulary**

Using the word bank on the next page, write the word that could replace the italicized word or words in each sentence. Use the Latin words in parentheses to help determine the meaning of the English words. Then write the English translation of each Latin word in the word bank:

1. The Cornelius family must travel on the Appian Way,
   because the carriage cannot cross rocky *ground*.   _____

2. Cornelius recommended protective *guardianship* to keep the
   visiting dignitary safe.   _____

3. Sextus found nothing but a *harmless* cat under the bed.   _____

4. Near Baiae, Lake Avernus gives off *harmful* sulfurous fumes.   _____

5. The emperor hopes to add new *land* to the empire of Rome. _____

6. Cornelius wishes to *limit* the freedom the boys have in the city. _____

7. Some snakes use poison, others *coil tightly around* their prey to kill it. _____

8. Aurelia has no *trust* in Titus as a chaperone for the boys. _____

9. The boys will *save* their energy for the visit to the Circus Maximus. _____

10. In the Roman Republic, the tribune had the power to *prohibit* actions of the Senate. _____

constrict (**stringere**) _____	territory (**terra**) _____
noxious (**nocēre**) _____	confidence (**cōnfīdere**) _____
veto (**vetāre**) _____	custody (**custōs**) _____
terrain (**terra**) _____	restrict (**stringere**) _____
conserve (**servāre**) _____	innocuous (**nocēre**) _____

Activity 26g Reading Latin

Look at the new vocabulary following this story. Then read the story, noting the use of forms of the demonstratives **hic** *and* **ille**. *Reread the Latin for comprehension. Answer the questions that follow the story with complete Latin sentences:*

"What's Wrong?"

Tertiā hōrā patruus Titus ad domum Cornēliānam advēnerat et in ātrium intrābat. Ibi Sextō et Cornēliae occurrit.

"Eho, līberī!" exclāmāvit. "Ecce illī vultūs miserī! Cūr in hīs sellīs sedētis? Nōnne in urbem exīre vultis? Cūr nōndum parātī estis?"

"Mārcus somnium malum heri nocte vīdit," inquit Cornēlia. "Nunc in urbem exīre nōn vult. Licēbitne nōbīs in urbem sine Mārcō īre?"

"Quid?" rogāvit Titus. "Quantum stultitiae! Mārce! Venī hūc!"

Mārcus tardē ātrium intrāvit et patruō appropinquāvit.

"Dīc mihi!" inquit patruus. "Quid in illō somniō vīdistī?"

"In illō somniō," respondit Mārcus, "per viās huius urbis cum Sextō ambulābam et tribus hominibus prope Circum occurrimus. Hī hominēs magnōs gladiōs ferēbant. Gladiōs strīnxērunt et clāmāvērunt, 'Rōmānōs nōn amāmus! Tē certē necābimus!' Suntne in hāc urbe tālēs hominēs scelestī?"

"Minimē, minimē!" dīxit Titus. "Nōlī sollicitus esse! Haec urbs magna et mīra est. In tantā urbe tamen sunt multī et variī hominēs. Sī vōs dīligenter cāvēbitis et prūdentēs eritis, incolumēs eritis. Hominēs scelestī vōs numquam vexābunt."

vultus, -ūs, m., *face, expression*
sella, -ae, f., *chair*
Quantum stultitiae! *What foolishness! What nonsense!*

varius, -a, -um, *different, varied*
prūdēns, prūdentis, *wise, sensible*

1. Quibus occurrit Titus, ubi ātrium intrāvit?

_____

2. Quō exīre volunt līberī?

_____

3. Quid in somniō vīdit Mārcus?

_____

4. Quid strīnxērunt hī hominēs?

_____

5. Quōs nōn amant hī hominēs scelestī?

_____

6. Quot et quālēs hominēs in tantā urbe sunt?

_____

A VISIT TO THE RACES

> *In addition to vocabulary and the story, the activities in this chapter focus on:*
> 1. the dative case with special intransitive verbs.
> 2. personal pronouns.
> 3. reflexive pronouns.
> 4. possessive adjectives.

Vocabulary

Activity 27a Vocabulary

Study the vocabulary list on pages 253–254 alone or with a partner. Go to the corresponding list on the Companion website where you will find a list of special intransitive verbs that take the dative case.

The Story

Activity 27b Sextus Tells It His Way

Sextus was so excited about the trip to the Circus that he couldn't wait to tell Cornelius all about the afternoon. Read the story below and give the English meanings of the Latin words in bold:

"Eugepae! Today everyone was **fēriātī = 1.** _____, so we were allowed

to go to the **lūdī circēnsēs = 2.** _____ in the **Circus Maximus**, which is a

3. _____. Thousands of people had come to watch the

charioteers race their **quadrīgae = 4.** _____, but despite the size of the crowd,

we got to sit right down by the **curriculum = 5.** _____. The track was

enormous, and the **spīna = 6.** _____ ran right down the center of it! It was

covered with shrines, altars, and statues, and at each end were the enormous **mētae =**

7. _____, that shone like gold in the sun! The charioteers all belonged to four

different **factiōnēs = 8.** _____, and they had different colored tunics. I cheered

for the **russātī = 9.** _____, Marcus cheered for the **albātī =**

10. _____, Cornēlia cheered for the **venetī = 11.** _____, and

Eucleides didn't cheer for anybody. Instead he just kept telling us for whom all the emperors had

cheered! That means nobody cheered for the **prasinī = 12.** _____. We were so

close to the track that I could even see **Caesar = 13.** _____ give the

signum = 14. _____ to start each race by dropping the **mappa =**

15. _____. I can't wait until we can go back again!

Activity 27c Questions about the Story

Answer in full Latin sentences these questions based on the story in Chapter 27:

1. Hodiē quō licet īre puerīs?

_____

_____

2. Quibuscum puerī ībunt?

_____

_____

3. Cūr Circus hodiē nōn clausus est?

_____

_____

4. Cūr puerī statim discēdere nōn possunt?

_____

_____

5. Quid audiunt puerī, ubi Circō appropinquant?

_____

_____

6. Quālis est turba?

_____

_____

7. Ubi Mārcus sedēre vult? Cūr?

_____

_____

8. Cūr Eucleidēs ibi sedēre nōn vult?

_____

_____

9. Quis venetīs favet?

_____

_____

10. Quōmodo aurīga russātus equōs agit?

_____

_____

11. Quīd facit aurīga Mārcī? Cūr?

_____

_____

12. Quid semper clāmant spectātōrēs?

_____

_____

13. Quī vincunt?

_____

_____

14. Cūr domum redīre necesse est?

_____

_____

15. Cūr Sextus domum redīre nōn vult?

_____

_____

Building the Meaning

Dative with Special Intransitive Verbs

Activity 27d Review of Verbs That Take the Dative Case

Choose a noun or phrase from the word bank on the next page that would make sense in each sentence. Fill in the blank in each sentence with the dative case form of the noun or phrase. Then translate the sentences:

1. Sī _____ nocueritis, pater eius certē vōs pūniet.

_____

_____

2. Ego _____ cōnfīdō. Ille līberōs bene custōdiet, quod eōs valdē amat.

_____

_____

3. Prīnceps ipse, ut omnēs bene scīmus, _____ favēre solet.

_____

_____

4. Sextā hōrā diēs erat calidus et nōs _____ appropinquābāmus.

_____

_____

5. Nōn licet _____ prope curriculum sedēre, nam ibi perīculum est magnum.

_____

_____

6. Sī extrā Cūriam manēbimus, fortasse _____ occurrēmus.

_____

_____

arcus Tiberiī	frāter Titus	prasinī
fīlius senātōris	līberī parvulī	prīnceps

Forms

Pronouns: 1st and 2nd Persons

Activity 27e Choosing the Correct 1st or 2nd Person Pronoun

Read the following English sentences. Determine the function of the word or phrase in bold type in each sentence. Then circle the form of the Latin pronoun that would replace it and correctly fit the grammar if the sentence were written in Latin:

1. Aurelia: I'm glad it was allowed **for you** to go to the Circus today, Cornelia.

tū / tibi / tē

2. Cornelia: I am glad, too, mother, but I'm sorry that you could not come **with us**.

nōbīscum / nōs / nōbīs

3. Aurelia: Did Eucleides watch **you** carefully?

vōbīs / tū / vōs

4. Cornelia: Yes, it was not permitted **for us** to sit near the racetrack.

nōs / nōbīs / nostrī

5. Aurelia: Whom did **you** favor?

tū / vōs / tē

6. Cornelia: **I** favored the blues.

ego / mihi / mē

7. Aurelia: Did Sextus annoy **you**?

tū / tibi / tē

8. Cornelia: No, he watched the horses and charioteers, and **we** all got along fine.

nōs / nostrī / nōbīs

9. Aurelia: I am glad that **you** all had fun.

tū / vōs / vōbīs

10. Cornelia: Thank you, mother, I am glad it was permitted **for me** to go.

mē / meī / mihi

Pronouns: 3rd Person

Activity 27f Choosing the Correct 3rd Person Pronoun

Read the following sentences. Complete the second sentence by filling in the blank with the proper form of the pronoun is, ea, id. Use the noun in bold type in the first sentence to determine the gender and number of the pronoun, but be sure to use the case that completes the meaning of the second sentence grammatically. Then translate the sentences:

1. "Illum **librum** legere volō," inquit Mārcus. "Da mihi _____!"

_____

2. "Māter, **Mārcus** hunc librum habēre vult. Eum _____ dare nōlō."

_____

_____

3. Ecce! Ego hanc **lectīcam** tibi condūxī. In _____ domum redīre potes.

_____

_____

4. Quandō Caesar **signum** dabit? Diū _____ exspectāvī.

_____

_____

5. **Aurīgae** russātī semper quadrīgās magnā arte agunt. Ego _____ hodiē faveō.

_____

_____

6. Sedēbimusne prope curriculum cum **patruō Titō**? Ita vērō! _____ amō.

_____

_____

7. **Amīcī** Titī sunt virī bonī. Fortasse mox cum _____ cēnābimus.

_____

_____

8. Vīdistisne in Forō **aedificia** mīra, puerī? Ita vērō! Eucleidēs _____ nōbīs dēmōnstrāvit.

_____

_____

9. **Līberōs** nōn videō quod in hortō sunt. Vōcēs _____ tamen audīre possum.

_____

_____

10. **Servī** nōs adiuvābant. Deinde caupō _____ cēnam nōbīs parāre iussit.

_____

Pronouns: Personal and Reflexive

Activity 27g Personal and Reflexive Pronouns

Fill in the blanks in the following sentences with the proper forms of pronouns to match the English cues. Read the sentences to determine which case to use. Circle all pronouns that are reflexive:

1. Nocuistīne _____, Sexte, ubi cecidistī? (yourself)

2. Minimē! _____ nōn nocuī. (myself)

3. Nocuitne _____ Mārcus? (himself)

4. Minimē! Nēmō _____ nocuit. (him)

5. Fēminae: _____ in aquā piscīnae vidēmus. (Ourselves)

6. Fēminae: _____ quoque, virī, in aquā piscīnae vidēre possumus. (You, pl.)

7. Virī: _____, fēminae, in aquā piscīnae vidēre possumus. (You, pl.)

8. Virī: _____ in aquā piscīnae vidēre nōn possumus. (Ourselves)

9. Virī _____ in aquā piscīnae vidēre possunt. (them, i.e., the women)

10. _____ tamen in aquā piscīnae vidēre nōn possunt. (Themselves)

11. Sextus _____ cōgitābat, "Sōlus esse nōlō." (with/to himself)

12. "Fortasse Mārcus _____ pilā lūdere vult." (with me)

13. "Laetus _____ pilā lūdam," respondit Mārcus. (with you)

14. "Ita _____ dēlectāre fortasse poterimus. (ourselves)

   dēlectō, -āre, -āvī, -ātus, *to please, delight, amuse*

Adjectives: Possessive

Activity 27h Possessives

Fill in the blanks with Latin words to match the English cues:

1. "Hic liber_____ est." inquit Cornēlia. (mine)

2. Mārcus librōs _____ legere heri volēbat. (his own)

3. Hodiē Mārcus librum _____ legere vult. (her)

4. "Estne hic liber _____, Cornēlia?" (your)

5. "Minimē. Liber _____ est." (his)

6. "Nōlīte nocēre amīcīs _____, puerī." (your)

7. "Amīcōs _____ cūrābimus, pater." (our)

8. Multī Rōmānī servīs _____ nōn cōnfīdunt. (their own)

9. "Cōnfīdisne servīs _____, Cornēlī?" (your)

10. "Servīs _____ cōnfīdō." (my)

Applying What You Have Learned

Activity 27i Writing the Language

Translate the following English sentences into Latin. Include all long marks. Use the stories and vocabulary lists in your textbook, as well as the vocabulary lists in this book, to help you:

1. Eucleidēs wanted to go to the Circus Maximus. He took the children with him.

_____

_____

2. Marcus favored the whites, but (his) sister (favored) the blues.

_____

3. "Alas!" Marcus shouted, "My charioteer fell!"

_____

4. The charioteer fell but hurt neither himself nor his horses.

_____

5. "Hurray!" shouted Cornelia, "Your charioteer and his horses are unhurt!"

_____

Activity 27j Expanding Your English Vocabulary

For each italicized English word, give the related Latin word and below it the meaning of that Latin word. Then complete each sentence by filling in a word at the right:

Latin Word
Meaning of the Latin Word   **If you ...**

1. _____   are *invincible*, you cannot
                                       be
_____   _____

2. _____   show your *favor* or support
                                       for one candidate in an
_____   election, that person is your
                                       _____ candidate.   _____

3. _____   have achieved a *victory* over
                                       your opponent, you have
_____   _____ him.   _____

4. _____   are *humiliated*, you are made
                                to feel _____, as if
_____   "cast on the ground."   _____

5. _____   belong to a *faction*, you are
                                  a member of a partisan
_____   _____, usually formed to   _____
                                  oppose the majority.

6. _____   *convince* people, you _____
                                  them over to your side.   _____

_____

7. _____   follow a university's
                                  curriculum, you follow its   _____

_____

8. _____   give the *sign* for the start
                                  of a race, you start the
_____   race with a prearranged   _____

9. _____   have an *albino* cat, you have a
                                  cat whose fur is
_____   _____

Activity 27k Reading Latin

Look at the new vocabulary on the next page. Then read the story, noting the forms of
pronouns and possessive adjectives. Reread the Latin for comprehension. Then mark whether
*each statement about the story is V = **Vērum** (True) or F = **Falsum** (False):*

More News for Flavia from Cornelia

Mē et puerōs ad lūdōs in Circō Maximō factōs herī Eucleidēs dūxit. Ubi

ē somnō surrēxī, puerī et Eucleidēs sē iam parāverant. Statim igitur Circum

petīvimus. Ubi eō pervēnimus, patruus noster cum suīs amīcīs iam prope

curriculum cōnsēderat. Quamquam prope curriculum sedēre nōbīs nōn licuit,

omnia tamen vidēre potuimus. Postquam aurīgae habēnās sūmpsērunt, Caesar

ipse signum mappā dedit. Quam celeriter equī cucurrērunt, nam aurīgae eōs

ferōciter verberābant!

Omnēs mulierēs, senātōrēs, cīvēs, servī factiōnibus suīs strēnuē favēbant.

Quam magnae erant vōcēs eōrum! Ego et puerī factiōnibus nostrīs favēbāmus.

Sextus, ille puer molestus, nōbīs identidem clāmābat, "Meī russātī semper vestrōs

aurīgās vincent!" Quamquam prīmō russātī eius vīcērunt, meī venetī saepe

vīcērunt. Albātī Mārcī nōn bene currēbant, et Mārcus miser sibi mussābat. Pauca

post certāmina tempus fuit discēdere. Dum domum redībāmus, puerī mē vexāre

temptābant, ut semper, sed eōs vītāre poteram.

Cum tū ad urbem vēneris, nōbīscum ad lūdōs circēnsēs fortasse īre poteris!

Licēbitne mox tibi Rōmam venīre? Sī māter tua tēcum vēnerit, laeta erit māter

mea quod eam vidēre vult.

Necesse est mihi cubitum īre. Valē, mea amīca.

prīmō, adv., *at first*   **paucī, -ae, -a,** *a few*   **certāmen, certāminis,** n., *contest*

1. Postquam Mārcus et Sextus sē quiētī dedērunt, puerī et Cornēlia cum
   Eucleide Circum petīvērunt.   V   F

2. Mārcus et Cornēlia patruum suum cum amīcīs eius sedentem in Circō cōnspexērunt.   V   F

3. Omnēs factiōnibus suīs favēbant.   V   F

4. Mārcus erat miser et Sextō mussābat.   V   F

5. Licuit līberīs omnia certāmina spectāre.   V   F

6. Dum līberī domum redībant, Cornēlia puerōs molestōs vītābat.   V   F

7. Cornēliae māter mātrem Flāviae vidēre vult.   V   F

VOCABULARY LISTED BY PART OF SPEECH

USING THESE VOCABULARY LISTS

The words in these chapter vocabulary lists are listed by part of speech. Use the lists to test yourself or work with a partner. Cut a notch in the top of a piece of paper. Cover the column of English meanings with the notched paper, allowing the notch in your paper to expose one Latin word at a time with its English meaning covered. Give the English meaning of that Latin word, and then move the notched paper down to expose the next Latin word. Check yourself as you go. Continue until you reach the bottom of the page. Then reverse the process and test yourself on your ability to give the Latin word for each English word you expose. Repeat the process as many times as necessary.

Latin words not in boldface are for recognition only. This means that you only need to be able to recognize the Latin word and give its English meaning.

Latin words in boldface are for mastery. You are expected to have a more active knowledge of these words. In addition to being able to give the English meaning for the Latin word, you should be able to give the Latin word for the English. Thus, when you expose the English word, you should be able to give its Latin equivalent. Further, you should be able to give whatever forms and information are contained in the entry for the Latin word. More forms and information will be contained in entries for Latin words beginning with Chapter 2.

Test yourself with these lists until you can recognize and give English meanings for all the Latin words and until you can give the Latin words and the forms and information contained in the entries for the words in boldface when you expose only the English meanings.

In the corresponding lists on the Companion website, we give additional lists of words for reveiw and consolidation for many of the chapters.

Chapter 1

NOUNS:

Italia	*Italy*
pictūra	*(a/the) picture*
puella	*(a/the) girl*
vīlla	*(a/the) country house*

ADJECTIVES:

altera	*second, one (of two), the other (of two), another*
laeta	*happy, glad*
Rōmāna	*Roman*
vīcīna	*neighboring, adjacent*

VERBS:

habitat	*(she/he) lives, is living, does live / dwells, is dwelling, does dwell*
sedet	*(she/he) sits, is sitting, does sit*
legit	*(she/he) reads, is reading, does read*
scrībit	*(she/he) writes, is writing, does write*
est	*(she/he/it) is*

WORDS AND PHRASES:

aestāte	*in the summer*
Cūr...?	*Why...?*
dum	*while*
Ecce!	*Look!*
et	*and*
etiam	*also*
iam	*now*
in	*in*
in Italiā	*in Italy*
in pictūrā	*in a/the picture*
in vīllā	*in a/the country house*
nōmine	*by name, named*
quae	*who*
Quid facit...?	*What is...doing? What does...do?*
Quis...?	*Who...?*
quod	*because*
sub arbore	*under a/the tree*
ubi	*where*
vīlla rūstica	*(a/the) country house and farm*

Chapter 2

NOUN (Singular/Plural):
In the story in Chapter 2, you saw both singular and plural forms of nouns and adjectives, so we list both forms here.

amīca / amīcae	*friend / friends*

ADJECTIVES (Singular/Plural):

dēfessa / dēfessae	*tired*
strēnua / strēnuae	*active, energetic*

ADVERBS:

hodiē	*today*
lentē	*slowly*
nōn	*not*
nōn iam	*no longer*
quoque	*also*
saepe	*often*
tandem	*at last, at length*

CONJUNCTION:

sed	*but*

VERBS (Singular/Plural):
In Chapter 2, you learned that there are different endings for singular and plural forms of verbs, namely, *-t* and *-nt*. To call your attention to this distinction, we give the singular and the plural forms here.

ambulat / ambulant	*(she/he) walks, is walking, does walk / (they) walk, are walking, do walk*
currit / currunt	*(she/he) runs, is running, does run / (they) run, are running, do run*
est / sunt	*(she/he/it) is / (they) are*

WORDS AND PHRASES:

ad vīllam rūsticam	*to/toward the country house and farm*
brevī tempore	*in a short time, soon*
eius	*her*
ex agrīs	*from/out of the fields*
in agrīs	*in the fields*
Quid faciunt...?	*What are...doing?*

Chapter 3

NOUNS (Singular/Plural):

We continue to give singular and plural forms of nouns.

fēmina / fēminae	*(a/the) woman / (the) women*
statua / statuae	*(a/the) statue / (the) statues*
amīcus / amīcī	*(a/the) friend / (the) friends*
puer / puerī	*(a/the) boy / (the) boys*
servus / servī	*(a/the) slave / (the) slaves*
vir / virī	*(a/the) man / (the) men*

ADJECTIVES (Singular/Plural):

For adjectives, we give the singular and plural forms that could be used in phrases such as the following:

puer <u>īrātus</u> / puerī <u>īrātī</u>
servus <u>īrātus</u> / servī <u>īrātī</u>
vir <u>īrātus</u> / virī <u>īrātī</u>
puella <u>īrāta</u> / puellae <u>īrātae</u>

alter	*second, one (of two), the other*
altera	*(of two), another*
Britannicus / Britannicī	*British*
Britannica / Britannicae	
īrātus / īrātī	*angry*
īrāta / īrātae	
multī	*many*
multae	
Rōmānus / Rōmānī	*Roman*
Rōmāna / Rōmānae	
sōlus / sōlī	*alone*
sōla / sōlae	

ADVERBS:

Minimē!	*No! Not at all!*
subitō	*suddenly*

VERBS (Singular/Plural):

We divide verbs into groups on the basis of the vowels (*a*, *e*, and *i* or *u*) that precede the
-*t* and **-*nt*** endings.

clāmat / clāmant	*(he/she) shouts, is shouting / (they) shout, are shouting*
labōrat / labōrant	*(he/she) works, is working / (they) work, are working*
rīdet / rīdent	*(he/she) laughs, is laughing, smiles, is smiling / (they) laugh, are laughing, smile, are smiling*
cadit / cadunt	*(he/she/it) falls, is falling / (they) fall, are falling*
gemit / gemunt	*(he/she) groans, is groaning / (they) groan, are groaning*

WORDS AND PHRASES:

Abīte, molestī!	*Go away, pests!*
ad piscīnam	*to the fishpond*
eādem	*the same*
ex hortō	*out of the garden*
in hortō	*in the garden*
in piscīnam	*into the fishpond*
in vīllīs rūsticīs	*in country houses*
Ita vērō!	*Yes! Indeed!*
quī	*who*

OTHER:

-ne	indicates a yes or no question

Chapter 4

NOUN (Singular/Plural Subject/Complement and Singular Direct Object):
In Chapter 4, you learned the ending *-m* for direct objects. To call your attention to this new ending, we give the direct object forms of nouns and adjectives (singular only).

rāmus / rāmī	*(a/the) branch / (the) branches*
rāmum	

NOUNS (Singular Subjects/Complements and Direct Objects):

fragor	*(a/the) crash, noise, din*
fragōrem	
vōx	*(a/the) voice*
vōcem	

ADJECTIVES (Singular/Plural Subjects/Complements and Singular Direct Objects):

īnfirmus / īnfirmī	*weak, shaky*
īnfirmum	
īnfirma / īnfirmae	
īnfirmam	
magnus / magnī	*big, great, large*
magnum	
magna / magnae	
magnam	
molestus / molestī	*troublesome, annoying*
molestum	
molesta / molestae	
molestam	
sollicitus / sollicitī	*anxious, worried*
sollicitum	
sollicita / sollicitae	
sollicitam	

PERSONAL PRONOUNS:
Pronouns are words that take the place of nouns, e.g., in English, *I, you, he, she, it, we, you,* and *they; me, you, him, her, it, us, you,* and *them*.

mē	*me* (direct object)
tē	*you* (direct object)
tū	*you* (subject)

ADVERBS:

fūrtim	*stealthily*
semper	*always*
tum	*at that moment, then*

CONJUNCTION:

igitur	*therefore*

VERBS (Singular/Plural):

amat / amant	*(he/she) likes, loves / (they) like, love*
appropinquat / appropinquant + ad + acc.	*(he/she) approaches, comes near (to) / (they) approach, come near (to)*
vexat / vexant	*(he/she) annoys / (they) annoy*
terret / terrent	*(he/she/it) frightens, terrifies / (they) frighten, terrify*
videt / vident	*(he/she) sees / (they) see*
ascendit / ascendunt	*(he/she) climbs / (they) climb*
cōnspicit / cōnspiciunt	*(he/she) catches sight of / (they) catch sight of*
audit / audiunt	*(he/she) hears, listens to / (they) hear, listen to*
dormit / dormiunt	*(he/she) sleeps / (they) sleep*

WORDS AND PHRASES:

Cavē!	*Be careful!*
Dēscende, Sexte!	*Come down, Sextus!*
magnā vōce	*in a loud voice*
nihil	*nothing*
Quālis...?	*What sort of...?*
Quō...?	*Where...to?*

Chapter 5

NOUNS (Singular/Plural Subjects/Complements and Singular Direct Objects):

lupus / lupī   *(a/the) wolf / (the) wolves*
lupum

rīvus / rīvī   *(a/the) stream / (the) streams*
rīvum

NOUN (Singular Subject/Complement and Direct Object):

clāmor   *(a/the) shout, shouting*
clāmōrem

ADJECTIVES (Singular/Plural Subjects/Complements and Singular Direct Objects):

calidus / calidī   *warm*
calidum

calida / calidae
calidam

frīgidus / frīgidī   *cool, cold*
frīgidum

frīgida / frīgidae
frīgidam

ignāvus / ignāvī   *cowardly, lazy*
ignāvum

ignāva / ignāvae
ignāvam

perterritus / perterritī   *frightened, terrified*
perterritum

perterrita / perterritae
perterritam

salvus / salvī   *safe*
salvum

salva / salvae
salvam

temerārius / temerāriī   *rash, reckless, bold*
temerārium

temerāria / temerāriae
temerāriam

PERSONAL PRONOUNS:

ego	*I*
eōs	*them*
eum	*him*

ADVERBS:

adhūc	*still*
ibi	*there* (location)
statim	*immediately*

CONJUNCTIONS:

neque...neque	*neither...nor*
sī	*if*
ubi	*where, when*

VERBS (Singular/Plural):

errat / errant	*(he/she) wanders / (they) wander*
respondet / respondent	*(he/she/it) replies / (they) reply*
timet / timent	*(he/she) fears, is afraid / (they) fear, are afraid*
petit / petunt	*(he/she) looks for, seeks / (they) look for, seek*
repellit / repellunt	*(he/she) drives off, drives back / (they) drive off, drive back*
arripit / arripiunt	*(he/she) grabs hold of, snatches / (they) grab hold of, snatch*
excipit / excipiunt	*(he/she) welcomes, receives / (they) welcome, receive*
advenit / adveniunt	*(he/she) reaches, arrives (at) / (they) reach, arrive (at)*

WORDS AND PHRASES:

ad puellās	*toward the girls*
ad vīllam	*at the country house*
ascendere	*to climb*
dēscendere	*to come/go down, climb down*
ē silvā	*out of the woods*
diēs	*(a/the) days*
exīre	*to go out*
Ferte auxilium!	*Bring help! Help!*
in silvam	*into the woods*
nōlō	*I do not wish, I do not want*
parās	*you prepare, get ready*
potest	*(he/she) is able, can*
prope	*near*
Quem...?	*Whom...?*
volō	*I wish, want*
vult	*(he/she) wishes, wants*

Chapter 6

NOUNS (Singular/Plural Subjects/Complements and Singular Direct Objects):

ancilla / ancillae ancillam	*slave-woman / slave-women*
aqua / aquae aquam	*water / waters*
cibus / cibī cibum	*food / foods*

NOUNS (Singular Subjects/Complements and Direct Objects):

māter, f. mātrem	*mother*
pater, m. patrem	*father*

ADVERBS:

etiam	*also, even*
mox	*soon, presently*
nōndum	*not yet*
nunc	*now*
strēnuē	*strenuously, hard*
tamen	*however*

CONJUNCTIONS:

neque	*and...not*
Review: neque...neque	*neither...nor*

VERBS (Singular/Plural):

observat / observant	*(he/she) watches / (they) watch*
portat / portant	*(he/she) carries / (they) carry*
pūrgat / pūrgant	*(he/she) cleans / (they) clean*
docet / docent	*(he/she/it) teaches / (they) teach*
lūcet	*it is light, it is day*
reprehendit / reprehendunt	*(he/she) blames, scolds, reproves / (they) blame, scold, reprove*
surgit / surgunt	*(he/she) gets up, rises / (they) get up, rise*

WORDS AND PHRASES:

adiuvāre	*to help*
coquere	*to cook*
cūrāre	*to look after, take care of*
ipsa	*she herself*
lānam trahunt	*(they) spin wool*
necesse est	*it is necessary*
omnēs	*all*
omnia quae	*everything that*
per vīllam	*through the country house*
Quī...?	*Who...?*

Chapter 7

NOUNS (Nominative Singular/Plural and Accusative Singular/Plural):

1st Declension:

epistula / epistulae	*letter / letters*
epistulam / epistulās	

2nd Declension:

nūntius / nūntiī	*messenger / messengers*
nūntium / nūntiōs	

3rd Declension:

prīnceps / prīncipēs, m.	*emperor / emperors*
prīncipem / prīncipēs	
senātor / senātōrēs, m.	*senator / senators*
senātōrem / senātōrēs	
urbs / urbēs, f.	*city / cities*
urbem / urbēs	

ADJECTIVES (Nominative Singular/Plural and Accusative Singular/Plural):

M	meus / meī	*my*
	meum / meōs	
F	mea / meae	
	meam / meās	
M	occupātus, occupātī	*busy*
	occupātum, occupātōs	
F	occupāta, occupātae	
	occupātam, occupātās	

PERSONAL PRONOUNS:

Review:

eās	*them* (feminine)
eōs	*them* (masculine)

INTERJECTIONS:

Ēheu!	*Alas!*
Eugepae!	*Hurray!*

VERBS (Singular/Plural):

revocat / revocant	*(he/she) recalls, calls back / (they) recall, call back*
salūtat / salūtant	*(he/she) greets, welcomes / (they) greet, welcome*
spectat / spectant	*(he/she) watches, looks at / (they) watch, look at*
dūcit / dūcunt	*(he/she) leads, takes, brings / (they) lead, take, bring*
trādit / trādunt	*(he/she) hands over / (they) hand over*
venit / veniunt	*(he/she) comes / (they) come*

WORDS AND PHRASES:

ad urbem	*to the city*
cōnsulere	*to consult*
inquit	*(he/she) says*
īre	*to go*
labōrantēs	*working*
Quōs...?	*Whom...?* (pl.)
redīre	*to return*
Rōmam	*to Rome*
Salvē!	*Greetings! Hello!*

Chapter 8

NOUNS (Nominative Singular/Plural and Accusative Singular/Plural):
1st Declension:

Britannia	*Britain*
Britanniam	
toga / togae	*toga / togas*
togam / togās	
tunica / tunicae	*tunic / tunics*
tunicam / tunicās	

3rd Declension:

nārrātor / nārrātōrēs, m.	*narrator / narrators*
nārrātōrem / nārrātōrēs	

PERSONAL PRONOUNS:
New and Review:

ego	*I*
mihi	*for me*
mē	*me*
tū	*you* (nom. sing.)
tē	*you* (acc. sing.)
eius	*of him/his, of her/her*
eum	*him*
nōs	*we* (nom.), *us* (acc.)
vōs	*you* (nom. or acc. pl.)
eōs	*them* (masc.)
eās	*them* (fem.)

ADVERBS:

celeriter	*quickly*
deinde	*then, next*
iam	*now, already*
iterum	*again, a second time*

CONJUNCTION:

nam	*for*

VERBS (Singular/Plural):

intrat / intrant	*(he/she) enters / (they) enter*
induit / induunt	*(he/she) puts on / (they) put on*

WORDS AND PHRASES:

Age! / Agite!	*Come on!*
cubiculum	*room, bedroom*
excitāre	*to rouse, wake (someone) up*
sedentēs	*sitting*
tempus	*time*

Chapter 9

NOUNS (Nominative Singular/Plural, Accusative Singular/Plural, and Ablative Singular/Plural):

1st Declension:

iānua / iānuae	*door / doors*
iānuam / iānuās	
iānuā / iānuīs	

3rd Declension:

iānitor / iānitōrēs	*doorkeeper / doorkeepers*
iānitōrem / iānitōrēs	
iānitōre / iānitōribus	

ADJECTIVES (Nominative Singular/Plural, Accusative Singular/Plural, and Ablative Singular/Plural):

M	miser / miserī	*unhappy, miserable, wretched*
	miserum / miserōs	
	miserō / miserīs	
F	misera / miserae	
	miseram / miserās	
	miserā / miserīs	
M	nūllus / nūllī	*no, not any*
	nūllum / nūllōs	
	nūllō / nūllīs	
F	nūlla / nūllae	
	nūllam / nūllās	
	nūllā / nūllīs	
M	sēmisomnus / sēmisomnī	*half-asleep*
	sēmisomnum / sēmisomnōs	
	sēmisomnō / sēmisomnīs	
F	sēmisomna / sēmisomnae	
	sēmisomnam / sēmisomnās	
	sēmisomnā / sēmisomnīs	
M	suus / suī	*his/her/its/their (own)*
	suum / suōs	
	suō / suīs	
F	sua / suae	
	suam / suās	
	suā / suīs	

M	tuus / tuī	*your* (sing.)
	tuum / tuōs	
	tuō / tuīs	
F	tua / tuae	
	tuam / tuās	
	tuā / tuīs	

PERSONAL PRONOUNS:

| eam | *her* |
| nōbīs | *for us* |

ADVERBS:

hīc	*here*
simul	*together, at the same time*
tacitē	*silently*

PREPOSITIONS:

Review:

ad + acc.	*to, toward, at, near*
ē/ex + abl.	*from, out of*
in + abl.	*in, on*
in + acc.	*into*
per + acc.	*through, along*
prope + acc.	*near*
sub + abl.	*under, beneath*

INTERJECTION:

| ō | *used with vocative and in interjections* |

VERBS (Singular/Plural):

excitat / excitant	*(he/she) rouses, wakes (someone) up / (they) rouse, wake (someone) up*
festīnat / festīnant	*(he/she) hurries / (they) hurry*
lacrimat / lacrimant	*(he/she) weeps, cries / (they) weep, cry*
temptat / temptant	*(he/she) tries / (they) try*
manet / manent	*(he/she) remains, stays / (they) remain, stay*
tacet / tacent	*(he/she) is quiet / (they) are quiet*
tenet / tenent	*(he/she) holds / (they) hold*
discēdit / discēdunt	*(he/she) goes away, departs / (they) go away, depart*
mittit / mittunt	*(he/she) sends / (they) send*
prōmittit / prōmittunt	*(he/she) promises / (they) promise*
nescit / nesciunt	*(he/she) is ignorant, does not know / (they) are ignorant, do not know*
abit / abeunt	*(he/she) goes away / (they) go away*

WORDS AND PHRASES:

ad iānuam	*at the door*
aliī...aliī...	*some...others...*
complexū	*in an embrace*
discēdere	*to go away*
lacrimāns	*weeping*
manēre	*to remain, stay*
mēcum	*with me*
Mitte!	*Send!*
nēmō	*no one*
nesciō	*I am ignorant, do not know*
Nōlī...excitāre!	*Don't wake...up!*
Ō mē miseram!	*Poor me! Oh dear me!*
prōmittis	*you* (sing.) *promise*
secundā hōrā	*at the second hour*
Tacē! / Tacēte!	*Be quiet!*
Valē! / Valēte!	*Goodbye!*
vōs omnēs	*you all, all of you*

Chapter 10

NOUNS (Nominative Singular/Plural, Accusative Singular/Plural, and Ablative Singular/Plural):

1st Declension:

cista / cistae cistam / cistās cistā / cistīs	*trunk, chest / trunks, chests*
palla / pallae pallam / pallās pallā / pallīs	*palla / pallas*
raeda / raedae raedam / raedās raedā / raedīs	*carriage / carriages*
stola / stolae stolam / stolās stolā / stolīs	*stola (a woman's outer garment) / stolas*
toga praetexta / togae praetextae togam praetextam / togās praetextās togā praetextā / togīs praetextīs	*toga with purple border / togas with purple borders*
via / viae viam / viās viā / viīs	*road / roads*

2nd Declension:

Cornēliī Cornēliōs Cornēliīs	*the Cornelii*
equus / equī equum / equōs equō / equīs	*horse / horses*
no singular / līberī no singular / līberōs no singular / līberīs	*children*
raedārius / raedāriī raedārium / raedāriōs raedāriō / raedāriīs	*coachman, driver / coachmen, drivers*

ADJECTIVES (Nominative Singular/Plural, Accusative Singular/Plural, and Ablative Singular/Plural):

M	alius / aliī alium / aliōs aliō / aliīs	*another, other / others*
F	alia / aliae aliam / aliās aliā / aliīs	
M	Cornēliānus / Cornēliānī Cornēliānum / Cornēliānōs Cornēliānō / Cornēliānīs	*belonging to Cornelius, Cornelian*
F	Cornēliāna / Cornēliānae Cornēliānam / Cornēliānās Cornēliānā / Cornēliānīs	
M	parātus / parātī parātum / parātōs parātō / parātīs	*ready, prepared*
F	parāta / parātae parātam / parātās parātā / parātīs	
M	scelestus / scelestī scelestum / scelestōs scelestō / scelestīs	*wicked*
F	scelesta / scelestae scelestam / scelestās scelestā / scelestīs	

ADVERBS:

crās	*tomorrow*
intereā	*meanwhile*

VERBS (1st Person Singular, Infinitive):

1st Conjugation:

exclāmō, exclāmāre	*to exclaim, shout out*
incitō, incitāre	*to spur on, urge on, drive*
stō, stāre	*to stand*

2nd Conjugation:

habeō, habēre	*to have, hold*
iubeō, iubēre	*to order, bid*
soleō, solēre + infin.	*to be accustomed (to), be in the habit (of)*

3rd Conjugation:

gerō, gerere	*to wear*
pōnō, pōnere	*to put, place*

3rd Conjugation (-iō):

iaciō, iacere	*to throw*

Imperatives (Irregular):

Verb	*Imperative*
dīcō, dīcere, *to say*	dīc! dīcite!
dūcō, dūcere, *to lead, take, bring*	dūc! dūcite!
faciō, facere, *to make, do*	fac! facite!
ferō, ferre, *to bring, carry, bear*	fer! ferte!

WORDS AND PHRASES:

baculum	*stick*
eō ipsō tempore	*at that very moment*
in itinere	***on a journey***
ipse	*himself*
servus quīdam	*a certain slave*
Ubi...?	***Where...?***

Chapter 11

NOUNS:

1st Declension:

ārea, -ae, f.	*open space, threshing floor*
fīlia, -ae, f.	*daughter*
īra, -ae, f.	*anger*
porta, -ae, f.	*gate*

2nd Declension:

dominus, -ī, m.	*master*
fīlius, -ī, m.	*son*
numerus, -ī, m.	*number*
vīlicus, -ī, m.	*overseer, farm manager*
vir, virī, m.	*man, husband*

3rd Declension:

frāter, frātris, m.	*brother*
māter, mātris, f.	*mother*
nox, noctis, f.	*night*
parēns, parentis, m./f.	*parent*
pater, patris, m.	*father*
soror, sorōris, f.	*sister*
uxor, uxōris, f.	*wife*

ADJECTIVE (Nominative Singular/Plural, Genitive Singular/Plural, Accusative Singular/Plural, and Ablative Singular/Plural):

M	plēnus / plēnī	*full*
	plēnī / plēnōrum	
	plēnum / plēnōs	
	plēnō / plēnīs	
F	plēna / plēnae	
	plēnae / plēnārum	
	plēnam / plēnās	
	plēnā / plēnīs	

CONJUNCTION:

quamquam	*although*

VERBS:

1st Conjugation:

cēlō, cēlāre	*to hide*
mussō, mussāre	*to mutter*
verberō, verberāre	*to beat*

3rd Conjugation (-iō):	effugiō, effugere	to flee, run away, escape
4th Conjugation:	impediō, impedīre	to hinder, prevent
Irregular:	absum, abesse	to be away, be absent

WORDS AND PHRASES:

id quod	that which, what
illā nocte	**that night**
redeunt	**(they) return**
sē cēlāre	**to hide (himself/herself)**
Via Appia	the Appian Way

Chapter 12

NOUNS:
1st Declension:

fossa, -ae, f.	*ditch*
vīnea, -ae, f.	*vineyard*

3rd Declension:

canis, canis, m./f.	*dog*

ADJECTIVES:
(Nominative Singular/Plural, Genitive Singular/Plural, Accusative Singular/Plural, and Ablative Singular/Plural):

M	bonus / bonī	*good*
	bonī / bonōrum	
	bonum / bonōs	
	bonō / bonīs	
F	bona / bonae	
	bonae / bonārum	
	bonam / bonās	
	bonā / bonīs	

(Nominative Singular/Plural):

M	immōbilis / immōbilēs	*motionless*
F	immōbilis / immōbilēs	

INTERROGATIVES:

Quandō...?	*When...?*
Quō īnstrūmentō...?	*With what instrument...? By what means...? How...?*
Quōcum...? or Quibuscum...?	*With whom...?*
Quōmodo...?	*In what manner...? How...?*
Ubi...?	*Where...?*
Unde...?	*From where...?*

PREPOSITION:

cum + abl.	*with*

VERBS:
1st Conjugation:

convocō, convocāre	*to call together*
lātrō, lātrāre	*to bark*
rogō, rogāre	*to ask*

3rd Conjugation:

trahō, trahere	*to drag*

3rd Conjugation (-iō):

olfaciō, olfacere	*to catch the scent of, smell*

4th Conjugation:

inveniō, invenīre	*to come upon, find*

Irregular:

ferō, ferre	*to bring, carry, bear*

WORDS AND PHRASES:

in fronte litterās inūrere	*to brand letters on the forehead*
tribus diēbus	*in three days*
tunicā	**by the tunic**
vēstīgia	**tracks, footprints, traces**

Chapter 13

NOUNS:

1st Declension:

aurīga, -ae, m.	*charioteer*
virga, -ae, f.	*stick, rod, switch*

2nd Declension:

rūsticus, -ī, m.	***peasant***
tabellārius, -ī, m.	***courier***

3rd Declension:

cīvis, cīvis, gen. pl., **cīvium,** m./f.	***citizen***
pars, partis, gen. pl., **partium,** f.	***part***
pēs, pedis, m.	***foot***

ADJECTIVES:
(Nominative Singular/Plural, Genitive Singular/Plural, Accusative Singular/Plural, and Ablative Singular/Plural):

M	fatuus / fatuī	*stupid*
	fatuī / fatuōrum	
	fatuum / fatuōs	
	fatuō / fatuīs	
F	fatua / fatuae	
	fatuae / fatuārum	
	fatuam / fatuās	
	fatuā / fatuīs	
M	**praeclārus / praeclārī**	***distinguished, famous***
	praeclārī / praeclārōrum	
	praeclārum / praeclārōs	
	praeclārō / praeclārīs	
F	**praeclāra / praeclārae**	
	praeclārae / praeclārārum	
	praeclāram / praeclārās	
	praeclārā / praeclārīs	
M	septimus	*seventh*
	septimī	
	septimum	
	septimō	
F	septima	
	septimae	
	septimam	
	septimā	

ADVERBS:

identidem	*again and again, repeatedly*
ferōciter	*fiercely*
Quam...!	*How...!*

PREPOSITION:

ab or **ā** + abl.	*from*

VERBS:

In Chapter 13 you learned about the imperfect tense, and in addition to the normal entries for verbs of the 1st, 2nd, and 3rd conjugations in this chapter we give 3rd person singular and plural imperfect forms of new verbs.

1st Conjugation:

vītō, vītāre	*to avoid*
vītābat / vītābant	*(he/she) was avoiding, kept avoiding / (they) were avoiding, kept avoiding*

3rd Conjugation:

quiēscō, quiēscere	*to rest*
quiēscēbat / quiēscēbant	*(he/she) was, kept resting / (they) were, kept resting*

Irregular:

sum, esse	*to be*
erat / erant	*(he/she/it) was / (they) were*
eō, īre	*to go*
ībat / ībant	*(he/she/it) was going, kept going / (they) were going, kept going*
possum, posse	*to be able; I can*
poterat / poterant	*(he/she/it) was able, could / (they) were able, could*
volō, velle	*to wish, want, be willing*
volēbat / volēbant	*(he/she) was wishing, wanted, was willing / (they) were wishing, wanted, were willing*

WORDS AND PHRASES:

Cavē!	*Be careful! Watch out (for)! Beware (of)!*
iter	*journey*
iter faciēbant	*(they) were traveling*
magnō rīsū	*with a loud laugh*
per viam	*along the road*
vehicula	*vehicles*

Chapter 14

NOUNS:
1st Declension:

culpa, -ae, f.	*fault, blame*

3rd Declension:

ars, artis, gen. pl., artium, f.	*skill*

ADJECTIVES:
(Nominative Singular/Plural, Genitive Singular/Plural, Accusative Singular/Plural, and Ablative Singular/Plural):

M	commōtus / commōtī	*moved*
	commōtī / commōtōrum	
	commōtum / commōtōs	
	commōtō / commōtīs	
F	commōta / commōtae	
	commōtae / commōtārum	
	commōtam / commōtās	
	commōtā / commōtīs	
M	no singular / cūnctī	*all*
	cūnctōrum	
	cūnctōs	
	cūnctīs	
F	cūnctae	
	cūnctārum	
	cūnctās	
	cūnctīs	
M	noster / nostrī	*our*
	nostrī / nostrōrum	
	nostrum / nostrōs	
	nostrō / nostrīs	
F	nostra / nostrae	
	nostrae / nostrārum	
	nostram / nostrās	
	nostrā / nostrīs	

(Nominative Singular/Plural):

M	incolumis, incolumēs	*unhurt, safe and sound*
F	incolumis, incolumēs	

ADVERBS:

celerrimē	*very fast*
frūstrā	*in vain*
placidē	*gently, peacefully*

VERBS:
1st Conjugation:

cessō, cessāre	*to be idle, do nothing*
interpellō, interpellāre	*to interrupt*

2nd Conjugation:

gaudeō, gaudēre	*to be glad, rejoice*
haereō, haerēre	*to stick*
moveō, movēre	*to move*

3rd Conjugation:

accidit	*(it) happens*
agō, agere	*to do, drive*
concidō, concidere	*to fall down*
dēvertō, dēvertere	*to turn aside*
extrahō, extrahere	*to drag out*

WORDS AND PHRASES:

cisium	*light two-wheeled carriage*
olīvētum	*olive grove*
perīculum	*danger*
quod	*which*
tuā culpā	*because of your fault, it's your fault that*
Tūne...spectābās?	*Were you watching?*

Chapter 15

NOUNS:
1st Declension:

rota, -ae, f.	*wheel*

2nd Declension:
Neuter Nouns:
New:

plaustrum, -ī, n.	*wagon, cart*
silentium, -ī, n.	*silence*

Review:

auxilium, -ī, n.	*help*
baculum, -ī, n.	*stick, staff*
cisium, -ī, n.	*light two-wheeled carriage*
cubiculum, -ī, n.	*room, bedroom*
olīvētum, -ī, n.	*olive grove*
perīculum, -ī, n.	*danger*
vehiculum, -ī, n.	*vehicle*
vēstīgium, -ī, n.	*track, footprint, trace*

3rd Declension:

bōs, bovis, m./f.	*ox, cow*
hominēs, hominum, m. pl.	*people*
nūbēs, nūbis, gen. pl., nūbium, f.	*cloud*
pulvis, pulveris, m.	*dust*

Neuter Nouns:
New:

murmur, murmuris, n.	*murmur, rumble*
onus, oneris, n.	*load, burden*

Review:

iter, itineris, n.	*journey*
nōmen, nōminis, n.	*name*
tempus, temporis, n.	*time*

ADJECTIVES:
(Nominative Singular/Plural, Genitive Singular/Plural, Accusative Singular/Plural, and Ablative Singular/Plural):

Since neuter nouns are formally introduced in Chapter 15, we give neuter forms of adjectives in addition to the masculine and feminine forms given previously.

M	longus / longī	*long*
	longī / longōrum	
	longum / longōs	
	longō / longīs	
F	longa / longae	
	longae / longārum	
	longam / longās	
	longā / longīs	

N	longum / longa	
	longī / longōrum	
	longum / longa	
	longō / longīs	
M	tardus / tardī	*slow*
	tardī / tardōrum	
	tardum / tardōs	
	tardō / tardīs	
F	tarda / tardae	
	tardae / tardārum	
	tardam / tardās	
	tardā / tardīs	
N	tardum / tarda	
	tardī / tardōrum	
	tardum / tarda	
	tardō / tardīs	

Roman Numerals and Numbers (this chapter and review):

I	ūnus	*one*
	ūna	
	ūnum	
II	duo	*two*
	duae	
	duo	
III	trēs	*three*
	trēs	
	tria	
IV	quattuor	*four*
V	quīnque	*five*
VI	sex	*six*
VII	septem	*seven*
VIII	octō	*eight*
IX	novem	*nine*
X	decem	*ten*
L	quīnquāgintā	*fifty*
C	centum	*a hundred*
D	quīngentī, -ae, -a	*five hundred*
M	mīlle	*a thousand*

ADVERBS:

diū	*for a long time*
fortasse	*perhaps*
praetereā	*besides*
procul	*in the distance, far off*
tantum	*only*

VERBS:

1st Conjugation:

exspectō, exspectāre	*to look out for, wait for*

2nd Conjugation:

appāreō, appārēre	*to appear*

Irregular:

praetereō, praeterīre	*to go past*

WORDS AND PHRASES:

illud	*that*
Neāpolim	*to Naples*
Quot...?	*How many...?*

Chapter 16

NOUNS:

1st Declension:

pila, -ae, f.	*ball*

2nd Declension:

animus, -ī, m.	*mind*
iocus, -ī, m.	*joke, prank*

3rd Declension:

hospes, hospitis, m./f.	*friend*

ADJECTIVES:

cārissimus, -a, -um	*dearest*
mortuus, -a, -um	*dead*
nōnus, -a, -um	*ninth*
novus, -a, -um	*new*

PERSONAL PRONOUNS:

eam	*her, it*
illa	*she*

ADVERB:

itaque	*and so, therefore*

CONJUNCTION:

ut	*as*

PREPOSITIONS:

apud + acc.	*at the house of, with*
dē + abl.	*down from, concerning, about*

VERBS:

1st Conjugation:

vocō, vocāre	*to call*

3rd Conjugation:

lūdō, lūdere	*to play*
relinquō, relinquere	*to leave behind*
vertō, vertere	*to turn*

3rd Conjugation (-iō):

excipiō, excipere	*to welcome, receive, catch*

4th Conjugation:

aperiō, aperīre	*to open*
feriō, ferīre	*to hit, strike*
sciō, scīre	*to know*

WORDS AND PHRASES:

alter...alterum	*the one...the other*
in animō habēre	*to intend*
nōbīscum	*with us*
per iocum	*as a prank*
pilā lūdere	*to play ball*
Sextum taedēbat	*it bored Sextus*
Vīsne...?	*Do you want...?*

Chapter 17

NOUNS:
1st Declension:

caupōna, -ae, f.	*inn*
domina, -ae, f.	*mistress, lady of the house*

2nd Declension:

aedificium, -ī, n.	*building*
caelum, -ī, n.	*sky*

3rd Declension:

caupō, caupōnis, m.	*innkeeper*

ADJECTIVES:

Graecus, -a, -um	*Greek*
perīculōsus, -a, -um	*dangerous*
ūndecimus, -a, -um	*eleventh*

VERBS:
1st Conjugation:

pernoctō, pernoctāre	*to spend the night*

3rd Conjugation:

advesperāscit, advesperāscere	*it gets dark*

4th Conjugation:

custōdiō, custōdīre	*to guard*

Irregular (Review):

eō, īre	*to go*
ferō, ferre	*to bring, carry, bear*
nōlō, nōlle	*not to wish, not to want, to be unwilling*
possum, posse	*to be able; I can*
sum, esse	*to be*
volō, velle	*to wish, want, be willing*

Chapter 18

NOUNS:
1st Declension:

cauda, -ae, f.	*tail*

2nd Declension:

lēgātus, -ī, m.	*envoy*

3rd Declension:

homō, hominis, m.	*man*
os, ossis, n.	*bone*
viātor, viātōris, m.	*traveler*

ADJECTIVES:
1st and 2nd Declension:

obēsus, -a, -um	*fat*

3rd Declension:
  New:

fortis, -is, -e	*brave, strong*

  Review:

brevis, -is, -e	*short*
immōbilis, -is, -e	*motionless*
incolumis, -is, -e	*unhurt, safe and sound*
omnis, -is, -e	*all, the whole, every, each*
Quālis, -is, -e...?	*What sort of...?*

ADVERBS:

modo	*only*
ōlim	*once (upon a time)*

CONJUNCTION:

nisi	*unless, if...not, except*

INTERJECTION:

Mehercule!	*By Hercules! Goodness me!*

VERBS:
1st Conjugation:

errō, errāre	*to wander, be mistaken*
laudō, laudāre	*to praise*

2nd Conjugation:

doleō, dolēre	*to be sad*

3rd Conjugation:

agnōscō, agnōscere	*to recognize*
extendō, extendere	*to hold out*
praecurrō, praecurrere	*to run ahead*

3rd Conjugation (-iō):

fugiō, fugere	*to flee*

WORDS AND PHRASES:

appāruit	*(he/she) appeared*
hī canēs	*these dogs*
lātrantēs	*barking*
manum	*hand*
nisi errō	*unless I am mistaken*
pernoctāvērunt	*(they) have spent the night*
Quid agis?	*How are you?*
revocāvit	*(he/she) called back*
sē praecipitant	*(they) hurl themselves, rush*
vesperī	*in the evening*

Chapter 19

NOUNS:
1st Declension:

cēna, -ae, f.	*dinner*

2nd Declension:

lectus, -ī, m.	*bed*

ADJECTIVES:
1st and 2nd Declension:

sordidus, -a, -um	*dirty*

PERSONAL PRONOUNS:

tibi	*to/for you* (sing.)
vōbīs	*to/for you* (pl.)

ADVERBS:

certē	*certainly*
valdē	*very, very much, exceedingly*
vehementer	*very much, violently, hard*

VERBS:
First Line: Present Tense 1st Person Singular and Infinitive
Second Line: Perfect Tense 3rd Person Singular / Plural

1st Conjugation:

cēnō, cēnāre	*to dine, eat dinner*
cēnāvit / cēnāvērunt	*(he/she) dined, ate dinner / (they) dined, ate dinner*
explicō, explicāre	*to explain*
explicāvit / explicāvērunt	*(he/she) explained / (they) explained*
vigilō, vigilāre	*to stay awake*
vigilāvit / vigilāvērunt	*(he/she) stayed awake / (they) stayed awake*

4th Conjugation:

ēsuriō, ēsurīre no perfect	*to be hungry*

Irregular:

eō, īre	*to go*
iit or īvit / iērunt or īvērunt	*(he/she) went / (they) went*

WORDS AND PHRASES:

Cornēliō	*for Cornelius*
cubitum īre	***to go to bed***
cui	*to whom, to him, to her*
hic lectus	***this bed***
hoc	***this***
melior	***better***
Nōnne...?	***Surely...?*** (introduces a question that expects the answer "yes")
Quid fēcit...?	***What did...do?***
rem explicāre	***to explain the situation***

Chapter 20

NOUNS:
1st Declension:

fābula, -ae, f.	*story*

3rd Declension:

mīles, mīlitis, m.	*soldier*

ADJECTIVES:
1st and 2nd Declension:

medius, -a, -um	*mid-, middle of*
nārrātus, -a, -um	*told*
optimus, -a, -um	*best, very good*

ADVERBS:

anteā	*previously, before*
attentē	*attentively, closely*
heri	*yesterday*
numquam	*never*
paulisper	*for a short time*

CONJUNCTIONS:

cnim	*for*
postquam	*after*

PREPOSITION:

post + acc.	*after*

VERBS:
1st Conjugation:

dēvorō, -āre, -āvī, -ātus	*to devour*
lavō, lavāre, lāvī, lautus	*to wash*
nārrō, -āre, -āvī, -ātus	*to tell (a story)*
necō, -āre, -āvī, -ātus	*to kill*

3rd Conjugation:

dīcō, dīcere, dīxī, dictus	*to say, tell*

WORDS AND PHRASES:

Estō!	*All right!*
hacc	*these things, this*
ille	*he*
in hanc caupōnam	*into this inn*
Licetne nōbīs...?	*Is it allowed for us...? May we...?*
media nox	*midnight*
vir optime	*sir*

Chapter 21

NOUNS:
1st Declension:

Asia, -ae, f.	*Asia (Roman province in western Asia Minor)*
culīna, -ae, f.	**kitchen**
Graecia, -ae, f.	*Greece*
innocentia, -ae, f.	*innocence*
pecūnia, -ae, f.	**money**
pīrāta, -ae, m.	*pirate*

2nd Declension:

aurum, -ī, n.	*gold*
crotalum, -ī, n.	*castanet*
somnium, -ī, n.	**dream**
somnus, -ī, m.	**sleep**

3rd Declension:

corpus, corporis, n.	**body**
fēlēs, fēlis, gen. pl., fēlium, f.	*cat*
Gādēs, Gādium, f. pl.	*Gades, Cadiz (a town in Spain)*
lībertās, lībertātis, f.	**freedom**
lūx, lūcis, f.	**light**
mors, mortis, gen. pl., **mortium,** f.	**death**
mūs, mūris, m.	*mouse*
saltātrīx, saltātrīcis, f.	*dancer*
stercus, stercoris, n.	*dung, manure*

ADJECTIVES:
1st and 2nd Declension:

invītus, -a, -um	**unwilling**
malus, -a, -um	**bad**
mortuus, -a, -um	**dead**
prīmus, -a, -um	**first**
timidus, -a, -um	*afraid, fearful, timid*
tōtus, -a, -um	**all, the whole**

PERSONAL PRONOUN:

eī	*to/for him, her, it*

ADVERBS:

ita	*thus, so, in this way*
māne	**early in the day, in the morning**
Quandō...?	*When...?*
sērō	**late**
suprā	**above, on top**

PREPOSITION:

praeter + acc.	*except*

VERBS:

1st Conjugation:

accūsō, -āre, -āvī, -ātus	*to accuse*
appellō, -āre, -āvī, -ātus	*to call, name*
cantō, -āre, -āvī, -ātus	*to sing*
cōgitō, -āre, -āvī, -ātus	*to think*
dō, dare, dedī, datus	*to give*
saltō, -āre, -āvī, -ātūrus	*to dance*
simulō, -āre, -āvī, -ātus	*to pretend*

2nd Conjugation:

removeō, removēre, remōvī, remōtus	*to remove, move aside*

3rd Conjugation:

emō, emere, ēmī, ēmptus	*to buy*
tremō, tremere, tremuī	*to tremble*

3rd Conjugation (-iō):

capiō, capere, cēpī, captus	*to take, catch, capture*
coniciō, conicere, coniēcī, coniectus	*to throw*
īnspiciō, īnspicere, īnspexī, īnspectus	*to examine*

4th Conjugation:

fīniō, -īre, -īvī, -ītus	*to finish*
obdormiō, -īre, -īvī, -ītūrus	*to go to sleep*
pūniō, -īre, -īvī, -ītus	*to punish*

WORDS AND PHRASES:

ad mortem	*to my death*
animum recuperāre	*to regain one's senses, wake up*
nihil malī	*nothing of a bad thing, there is nothing wrong*
prīmā lūce	*at dawn*
sonitus	*sound*
vidētur	*(he/she/it) seems*

Chapter 22

NOUNS:
1st Declension:

habēnae, -ārum, f. pl.   *reins*

2nd Declension:

mandātum, -ī, n.   *order, instruction*
patruus, -ī, m.   *uncle*
sepulcrum, -ī, n.   *tomb*

3rd Declension:

mercātor, mercātōris, m.   *merchant*
ōrātor, ōrātōris, m.   *orator, speaker*
terror, terrōris, m.   *terror, fear*

ADJECTIVES:
1st and 2nd Declension:

nocturnus, -a, -um   *happening during the night*
vester, vestra, vestrum   *your* (pl.)

3rd Declension:

immemor, immemoris + gen.   *forgetful*
ingēns, ingentis   *huge*

PERSONAL PRONOUNS:

eī, eae   *they*
eīs   *to/for them*

ADVERB:

bene   *well*

CONJUNCTIONS:

atque   *and, and also*
cum   *when*

PREPOSITION:

intrā + acc.   *inside*

VERBS:
1st Conjugation:

mōnstrō, -āre, -āvī, -ātus   *to show*
stō, stāre, stetī, statūrus   *to stand*

2nd Conjugation:

admoveō, admovēre, admōvī, admōtus   *to move toward*

244 VOCABULARY LIST

3rd Conjugation:

ascendō, ascendere, ascendī, ascēnsus	*to climb, climb into (a carriage)*
cadō, cadere, cecidī, cāsūrus	*to fall*
discēdō, discēdere, discessī, discessūrus	*to go away, depart*
sūmō, sūmere, sūmpsī, sūmptus	*to take, take up, pick up*
trādō, trādere, trādidī, trāditus	*to hand over*

3rd Conjugation (-iō):

excipiō, excipere, excēpī, exceptus	*to welcome, receive, catch*

WORDS AND PHRASES:

auxiliō	*with the help*
Cuius...?	*Whose...?* (sing.)
illud	*that*
sē parāre	*to prepare oneself, get ready*

Chapter 23

NOUNS:
1st Declension:

Cūria, -ae, f.	*Senate House*
lectīca, -ae, f.	*litter*
turba, -ae, f.	*crowd, mob*

2nd Declension:

gaudium, -ī, n.	*joy*
lectīcārius, -ī, m.	*litter-bearer*
mūrus, -ī, m.	*wall*

3rd Declension:

imber, imbris, gen. pl., **imbrium,** m.	*rain*
multitūdō, multitūdinis, f.	*crowd*
pōns, pontis, gen. pl., **pontium,** m.	*bridge*
quiēs, quiētis, f.	*rest*

ADJECTIVES:
1st and 2nd Declension:

maximus, -a, -um	*greatest, very great, very large*
mīrus, -a, -um	*wonderful, marvelous, strange*
rīmōsus, -a, -um	*full of cracks, leaky*
stultus, -a, -um	*stupid, foolish*

3rd Declension:

tālis, -is, -e	*such, like this, of this kind*

ADVERBS:

eō	*there, to that place*
hūc illūc	*here and there, this way and that*
illūc	*there, to that place*
interdiū	*during the day, by day*
prīmum	*first*
satis*	*enough*
undique	*on all sides, from all sides*

*adverb or indeclinable substantive

CONJUNCTION:

at	*but*

PREPOSITIONS:

extrā + acc.	*outside*
suprā + acc.	*above*

VERBS:

1st Conjugation:

vīsitō, -āre, -āvī, -ātus	*to visit*

2nd Conjugation:

caveō, cavēre, cāvī, cautus	*to be careful, watch out (for), beware (of)*
maneō, manēre, mānsī, mānsus	*to remain, stay, wait (for)*
stupeō, -ēre, -uī	*to be amazed, gape*

3rd Conjugation:

agō, agere, ēgī, āctus	*to do, drive*
colō, colere, coluī, cultus	*to cultivate*
condūcō, condūcere, condūxī, conductus	*to hire*
cōnsīdō, cōnsīdere, cōnsēdī	*to sit down*
cōnstituō, cōnstituere, cōnstituī, cōnstitūtus	*to decide*
currō, currere, cucurrī, cursūrus	*to run*
dēscendō, dēscendere, dēscendī, dēscēnsūrus	*to come/go down, climb down*
induō, induere, induī, indūtus	*to put on*
pluit, pluere, pluit	*it rains, is raining* (usually found only in 3rd singular)
quiēscō, quiēscere, quiēvī, quiētūrus	*to rest, keep quiet*

3rd Conjugation (-iō):

faciō, facere, fēcī, factus	*to make, do*

4th Conjugation:

adveniō, advenīre, advēnī, adventūrus	*to reach, arrive (at)*

Irregular:

exeō, exīre, exiī or exīvī, exitūrus	*to go out*
redeō, redīre, rediī or redīvī, reditūrus	*to return, go back*

WORDS AND PHRASES:

aquaeductus	*aqueduct*
Cavē imbrem!	*Watch out for the rain!*
Circus Maximus	*the Circus Maximus (a stadium in Rome)*
domum	*homeward, home*
domus	*house, home*
ē domō	*out of the house*
exstantem	*standing out, towering*
multa et mīra	*many wonderful things*
satis temporis	*enough of time, enough time*
sē lāvit	*(he/she) washed*
sē quiētī dare	*to rest*
strepitus	*noise, clattering*

Chapter 24

NOUNS:
2nd Declension:

liber, librī, m.	*book*
lūdī, -ōrum, m. pl.	*games*

3rd Declension:

labor, labōris, m.	*work, toil*
mōlēs, mōlis, gen. pl., mōlium, f.	*mass, huge bulk*
mōns, montis, gen. pl., montium, m.	*mountain, hill*

ADJECTIVES:
1st and 2nd Declension:

attonitus, -a, -um	*astonished, astounded*
clausus, -a, -um	*shut, closed*
magnificus, -a, -um	*magnificent*
tantus, -a, -um	*so great, such a big*

ADVERB:

vix	*scarcely, with difficulty*

CONJUNCTION:

simulac	*as soon as*

VERBS:
1st Conjugation:

aedificō, -āre, -āvī, -ātus	*to build*
dēmōnstrō, -āre, -āvī, -ātus	*to show*

2nd Conjugation:

licet, licēre, licuit + dat.	*it is allowed* (usually found only in 3rd person singular and infinitive)
moveō, movēre, mōvī, mōtus	*to move*

3rd Conjugation:

legō, legere, lēgī, lēctus	*to read*
occurrō, occurrere, occurrī, occursūrus + dat.	*to meet, encounter*
scrībō, scrībere, scrīpsī, scrīptus	*to write*

Irregular:

circumeō, circumīre, circumiī or circumīvī, circumitus	*to go around*

WORDS AND PHRASES:

aestū	*from the heat*
arcus	***arch***
Mōns Palātīnus, Montis Palātīnī, m.	*the Palatine Hill*
quem, acc. sing.	*whom, which, that*

Chapter 25

NOUNS:
1st Declension:

causa, -ae, f.	*reason*
poēta, -ae, m.	*poet*
taberna, -ae, f.	*shop*

2nd Declension:

amphitheātrum, -ī, n.	*amphitheater*
Forum, -ī, n.	*the Forum (city center of Rome)*
patrōnus, -ī, m.	*patron*
stilus, -ī, m.	*pen*
vīnum, -ī, n.	*wine*

3rd Declension:

caput, capitis, n.	*head*
cliēns, clientis, gen. pl., clientium, m.	*client, dependent*
lapis, lapidis, m.	*stone*
postis, postis, gen. pl., postium, m.	*doorpost*

4th Declension:
New and Review:

aestus, -ūs, m.	*heat*
aquaeductus, -ūs, m.	*aqueduct*
arcus, -ūs, m.	*arch*
complexus, -ūs, m.	*embrace*
domus, -ūs, f.	*house, home*
manus, -ūs, f.	*hand*
(25) reditus, -ūs, m.	*return*
rīsus, -ūs, m.	*smile, laugh*
(25) **senātus, -ūs,** m.	*Senate*
sonitus, -ūs, m.	*sound*
strepitus, -ūs, m.	*noise, clattering*
(25) **tumultus, -ūs,** m.	*uproar, commotion*

5th Declension:
Review:

diēs, diēī, m.	*day*
rēs, reī, f.	*thing, matter, situation*

ADJECTIVES:
1st and 2nd Declension:

aureus, -a, -um	*golden*
excitātus, -a, -um	*wakened, aroused*
oppressus, -a, -um	*crushed*
quadrātus, -a, -um	*squared*
tertius, -a, -um	*third*

PERSONAL PRONOUN:

eōrum	*of them, their*

ADVERB:

abhinc	*ago, previously*

INTERJECTION:

Eho!	*Hey!*

VERBS:
2nd Conjugation:

teneō, tenēre, tenuī, tentus	*to hold*

3rd Conjugation:

stertō, stertere, stertuī	*to snore*
trahō, trahere, trāxī, tractus	*to drag, pull*

3rd Conjugation (-iō):

cōnficiō, cōnficere, cōnfēcī, cōnfectus	*to finish*
fugiō, fugere, fūgī, fugitūrus	*to flee*

4th Conjugation:

perveniō, pervenīre, pervēnī, perventūrus + ad + acc.	*to arrive (at), reach*

Irregular:

absum, abesse, āfuī, āfutūrus	*to be away, be absent, be distant*

WORDS AND PHRASES:

abhinc duās hōrās	*two hours ago*
ad tabernam quandam	*to a certain shop*
aliquid	*something*
dē omnibus rēbus	*about everything*
Domus Aurea	*(Nero's) Golden House*
eō diē	*on that day*
hic	*this man, the latter*
huius	*of this*
illī	*those men, the former*
quās (f., acc., pl.)	*whom, which, that*
quod (n., nom. or acc., sing.)	*which, that*
sequentēs	*following*

Chapter 26

NOUNS:
1st Declension:

terra, -ae, f.	*earth, ground*

2nd Declension:

ātrium, -ī, n.	***atrium, main room***
bona, -ōrum, n. pl.	***goods, possessions***
captīvus, -ī, m.	*prisoner*
colloquium, - ī, n.	*conversation*
gladius, -ī, m.	***sword***
lūdus, -ī, m.	***school***
lutum, -ī, n.	*mud*
oculus, -ī, m.	***eye***
tablīnum, -ī, n.	***study***

3rd Declension:

coniūnx, coniugis, m./f.	***husband, wife***
custōs, custōdis, m.	***guard***
ōrātiō, ōrātiōnis, f.	***oration, speech***
praedō, praedōnis, m.	***robber***

4th Declension:

metus, -ūs, m.	***fear***

ADJECTIVES:
1st and 2nd Declension:

antīquus, -a, -um	*ancient*
parvulus, -a, -um	*small, little*
quīntus, -a, -um	*fifth*
verbōsus, -a, -um	*talkative*

DEMONSTRATIVE ADJECTIVES AND PRONOUNS:

hic, haec, hoc	***this, the latter***
ille, illa, illud	***that, he, she, it, the former***

ADVERBS:

aliter	*otherwise*
nōnnumquam	***sometimes***
postrīdiē	***on the following day***

CONJUNCTIONS:

aut...aut...	*either...or...*
nisi	***unless, if...not, except***
ut	*as*

PREPOSITIONS:

apud + acc.	*at the house of, with, in front of, before*
propter + acc.	*on account of, because of*
sine + abl.	*without*

VERBS:
1st Conjugation:

dēsīderō, -āre, -āvī, -ātus	*to long for, miss*
servō, -āre, -āvī, -ātus	*to save*
vetō, vetāre, vetuī, vetitus	*to forbid*

2nd Conjugation:

dēbeō, -ēre, -uī, -itūrus + inf.	*ought*
iaceō, -ēre, -uī, -itūrus	*to lie, be lying down*
noceō, -ēre, -uī, -itūrus + dat.	*to do harm (to), harm*

3rd Conjugation:

accidit, accidere, accidit	*(it) happens*
claudō, claudere, clausī, clausus	*to shut*
cōnfīdō, cōnfidere + dat.	*to give trust (to), trust*
stringō, stringere, strīnxī, strictus	*to draw* (e.g., a sword)

3rd Conjugation (-iō):

arripiō, arripere, arripuī, arreptus	*to grab hold of, snatch, seize*

4th Conjugation:

aperiō, aperīre, aperuī, apertus	*to open*
sciō, scīre, scīvī, scītus	*to know*

Irregular:

adsum, adesse, adfuī, adfutūrus	*to be present*

WORDS AND PHRASES:

clāmantem	*shouting*
domī	*at home*
Grātiās tibi agō!	*I thank you! Thank you!*
Mōns Vesuvius, Montis Vesuviī, m.	*Mount Vesuvius (a volcano in Southern Italy)*
ōrātiōnem habēre	*to deliver a speech*
sī vīs	*if you wish, please*
ut Mārcō vidēbātur	*as it seemed to Marcus, as Marcus thought*

Chapter 27

NOUNS:
1st Declension:

fēriae, -ārum, f. pl.	*holiday, festival day*
mappa, -ae, f.	*napkin, white cloth*
mēta, -ae, f.	*mark, goal, turning post*
quadrīgae, -ārum, f. pl.	*team of four horses, chariot*
spīna, -ae, f.	*barrier (of a racetrack)*

2nd Declension:

curriculum, -ī, n.	*racetrack*
signum, -ī, n.	*signal*

3rd Declension:

Caesar, Caesaris, m.	*Caesar, emperor*
factiō, factiōnis, f.	*company (of charioteers)*
mulier, mulieris, f.	***woman***
spectātor, spectātōris, m.	*spectator*
victor, victōris, m.	*conqueror, victor*

ADJECTIVES:
1st and 2nd Declension:

albātus, -a, -um	*white*
fēriātus, -a, -um	*celebrating a holiday*
prasinus, -a, -um	*green*
russātus, -a, -um	*red*
venetus, -a, -um	*blue*

Possessive:

meus, -a, -um	***my, my own, mine***
tuus, -a, -um	***your, your own, yours*** (sing.)
suus, -a, -um (reflexive only)	***his own, her own, its own***
noster, nostra, nostrum	***our, our own, ours***
vester, vestra, vestrum	***your, your own, yours*** (pl.)
suus, -a, -um (reflexive only)	***their own***

3rd Declension:

circēnsis, -is, -e	*in/of the circus*

PERSONAL PRONOUNS:

ego	*I*
tū	*you* (sing.)
is, ea, id	*he, she, it*
nōs	*we*
vōs	*you* (pl.)
eī, eae, ea	*they*

Reflexive:

suī (gen.), **sibi** (dat.), **sē** (acc.), **sē** (abl.)	*himself, herself, oneself, itself, themselves*

VERBS:

2nd Conjugation:

faveō, favēre, fāvī, fautūrus + dat.	*to give favor (to), favor, support*

3rd Conjugation:

dēvertō, dēvertere, dēvertī, dēversus	*to turn aside*
vincō, vincere, vīcī, victus	*to conquer, win*

WORDS AND PHRASES:

humī	*on the ground*
lūdī circēnsēs, lūdōrum circēnsium, m. pl.	*games in the circus, chariot races*

PREFIXES:

ab-, abs-, ā-	*away, from*
ad-	*toward, to*
circum-	*around*
con-	*along with, together* (or simply to emphasize)
dē-	*down, down from*
dis-, dī-	*apart, in different directions*
ex-, ē-	*out, out of*
in-	*into, in, on*
inter-	*between*
per-	*through* (or simply to emphasize)
prae-	*in front, ahead*
praeter-	*past, beyond*
prō-, prōd-	*forward*
re-, red-	*back, again*
sub-	*under, below*
trāns-, trā-	*across*